"What I love about Yuloff Creative is that they become an in-house agency (marketing department) for small business owners. I think that's a brilliant idea. They think as if they are the small business owner's partner. They are true mentors and coaches that are truly looking out for the best interests of their clients. Over thirty years together, there's some wisdom going on here. You gotta check them out. Hank and Sharyn Yuloff, you guys are amazing. I'll see them in Sedona, you guys should make that contact right now too."

—Kevin Harrington, Original Shark on *Shark Tank*,
Creator of AsSeenOnTV.com

". . . Sharyn and Hank have guided me to more solutions and adaptations than I have worked out by myself over the length of years! No matter how savvy you are, we can always improve, and having *two* additional experienced perspectives will always hasten you towards your goals faster than anyone can on their own. They are the ideal examples of everything you'd need in a good coach: encouraging, succinct and clear, keen enough to catch the things we all miss, the right balance of teamwork . . . and of course, their special brand of inspiration that empowers us to really push ourselves, without feeling overwhelmed. Invest in their coaching. You won't regret it!"

—Emily Wilson, Professional Photographer

"Hank and Sharyn have patience and skill with mentoring a new business owner. They keep the information lighthearted, clear, and informative. All while keeping me accountable and offering doable steps which have proven to be productive and profitable! Following their suggestions has saved me time and money. This is only the beginning; I plan on years of successful partnering with this creative duo."

—Valerie M. Luna, CH.t, LunaHypnotherapy.com

"Nosso primeiro contato com o Time da Yuloff Creative não poderia ter vindo num momento mais crucial para o nosso negócio: no meio da pandemia. Naquele ponto, estávamos trabalhando para servir e criar oportunidades de vendas com os clientes que tínhamos, mas uma dificuldade enorme de expandir nossa clientela, principalmente no mercado Canadense, que era nosso principal foco. Hank e Sharyn traçaram um plano simples e eficaz que trouxe resultados imediatos para a Nova Idea, e podemos dizer com confiança que a nossa parceria com a Yuloff Creative foi e está sendo um sucesso."

—Eduardo DaSilveira, Founder, NovaIdeaInc.com

"The Yuloffs *way* over delivered on every promise. Hank and Sharyn are the best. Even before I hired them, they had given me more value than others I had tried."

—Joshua Dunn, Creator of the
Dunn Method to Avoid Carpal Tunnel Surgery

"Yuloff Creative is excellent at helping small businesses make the most of their marketing time and dollars. Sharyn and Hank stay up to date on what works *now*, not what worked five years ago. That's essential as things change rapidly in this technological age. And a huge plus: they're incredibly fun! . . . They're excellent connectors, so you want them in your network. You'll be glad you work with them."

—Will Bowers, Legal Shield, WilBowers.WeAreLegalShield.com

"I have learned so very much from Hank and Sharyn. Well worth every penny, every second. You should hire these people; they are well worth it and they are going to make your business grow beyond belief."

—Heather Parris, Self Propelled Tours Sedona

"Sharyn and Hank are true experts in marketing for small businesses. And as an added bonus, they are two of the most genuine, heart-centered speakers, coaches, consultants you could ever work with. If you"re ready to take your life and business to higher levels with continuous growth and improvement, then you must work with Yuloff Creative today!"

—Melissa Camacho, Acu-Sedona.com

"This couple is very informative! Amazingly professional, helpful and all around good people! You meet them once and you feel like you are family! I cannot express the gratitude I have towards their goal of helping small businesses like ours!

—Ryan Taylor, The City Locksmith

"Sharyn and Hank are so easy to work with and are amazing people. You can't go wrong with this dynamic duo!

Melissa Papke, broughtonHOTELS

"During business in good times or in difficult times with challenges, Sharyn and Hank Yuloff do an excellent job of supporting and educating their clients.

—Mary Laff, Laff Financial

"Sharyn and Hank are enthusiastic, knowledgeable, and genuine. They are a tremendous asset to any business. I highly recommend them."

—Jennifer Mogan, Park Place Payments

THE MARKETING CHECKLIST 4

THE MARKETING CHECKLIST 4

Your Guide for Overwhelmed

and Overthinking Entrepreneurs

Hank and Sharyn Yuloff

Naked Book Publishing

can generally expect from the information. No representation in any part of this information materials and/or seminar training are guarantees or promises for actual performance. Any statements, strategies, concepts, techniques, exercises and ideas in the information, materials and/or seminar training offered are simply opinion or experience, and thus should not be misinterpreted as promises, typical results or guarantees (expressed or implied). The author and publisher (Henry "Hank" Yuloff, Sharyn Yuloff, Naked Book Publishing nor any of their representatives) shall in no way, under any circumstances, be held liable to any party (or third party) for any direct, indirect, punitive, special, incidental or other consequential damages arising directly or indirectly from any use of books, materials and/or seminar trainings, which is provided "as is," and without warranties.

PRINTED IN THE UNITED STATES OF AMERICA

Contents

Preface *xiii*

Introduction: How to Use This Book *1*

Part 1   **The Concept of Overthinking, Being Overwhelmed, and How to Improve Your Mindset to Improve Your Sales and Marketing** *5*

Chapter 1   Your Warmup! 10 Easy Marketing Tips *7*
Chapter 2   Do You Have the Mindset of the Technician That Saved Fed Ex? *11*
Chapter 3   Starting Your New Business . . . or . . . Catching What You Missed the First Time *13*
Chapter 4   Starting Your New Business . . . or . . . Catching What You Missed the First Time—The Sequel *17*
Chapter 5   12 Effective Management Principles *25*
Chapter 6   Getting Paid What You're Worth—5 Rules of Pricing *27*
Chapter 7   Can You Do It for Less? I'll Be Your Best Customer *31*
Chapter 8   Help! I'm an Introvert Stuck in an Extrovert's Body! *35*
Chapter 9   Overthinking in Your Business: What Causes It *41*
Chapter 10   Overthinking in Your Business: Ways to Halt the Irrational Desire to Overthink Everything *45*
Chapter 11   Your Sales Cycle: 10 Cautionary Tales to Improve Your Sales Process without Overthinking It *51*

Part 2   **Nuts and Bolts of How to Stop Overthinking Your Sales and Marketing** *59*

Chapter 12   The 5 Questions Most Small Business Owners Ask about Branding *61*

Chapter 13   What Are the 12 Types of Videos You Can Create Now   *65*
Chapter 14   Tips for Making Your Video Backgrounds Better   *67*
Chapter 15   Your Overthinkers Guide to AI and Writing   *71*
Chapter 16   The Power of Your Frequently Asked Questions   *73*
Chapter 17   26 Ways to Repurpose Your Content and Increase Your Sales   *79*
Chapter 18   Here Are 10 Prospecting Mistakes You Are Probably Making Right Now   *85*
Chapter 19   Lack of Follow Up Is How They Lost the Sale   *91*
Chapter 20   (An Exciting Way) or (How) to Improve Your Follow Up and Productivity   *97*
Chapter 21   How to Create Your Client Retention Plan   *101*
Chapter 22   7 Simple Ways to Get to Know Your Customers Better   *105*
Chapter 23   14 Ways to Show Your Clients Some Love   *109*
Chapter 24   How to Pivot Your Business to Generate Sales During a Shock to Society   *113*
Epilogue   Final Thought to (Over)Think About   *119*

Our Story—Our Mission—Our Vision—Our Whys   *123*
The Answers to Questions That We Hear All the Time   *131*

Are You Ready to Energize Your Group's Meetings?

From 20 to 2,000

Book Sharyn and Hank!

"They're easy to work with and always deliver exactly what our attendees need. You will enjoy working with them." - S.C.O.R.E. - Los Angeles

"Every time I have brought them in to speak they have delivered above and beyond my expectations." - Brett Labit - WEVO Global

Call Now and Reserve Your Dates!
Info@YuloffCreative.com 800-705-4265

"America's #1 Coaching Team for Small Business Marketing!"

Preface

"Coaching is unlocking a person's potential to maximize their own performance. It's helping them to learn rather than teaching them."
Tim Gallwey, Sports Methodology Coach

"A coach is someone who tells you what you don't want to hear, who has you see what you don't want to see, so you can be who you always knew you could be."
Tom Landry, NFL Hall of Fame Coach

"Probably my best quality as a coach is that I ask a lot of engaging questions and let the person come up with the answer."
Phil Dixon

We are only able to do the things discussed in these quotations because of our clients, both past and present. We thank you for your trust and we promise to continue to work our tails off for you.

We welcome you to the latest addition to The Marketing Checklist series of business books. Like our other books, this one is made up of a combination of reworked, updated, and edited blog posts and special reports, as well as additional original content created to match the subject matter of this book.

Books are continuously added to this series because we know that you, our audience members, have a sincere desire to improve your small business and we are here to help you. We're the go-to small business coaches for highly motivated entrepreneurs just like you. And, we are especially effective for the overwhelmed overthinkers, no matter what your industry.

For most entrepreneurs, the three hardest areas to control and improve in their business are the areas where we focus—your marketing and messaging, your sales abilities, and your human resources and relationships. For the incredible small business owners who find us, we create a custom business coaching package that looks at deeper fundamentals of your business, such as your business model, your operations, your profit margins, and your marketing plan.

For all these areas, it's not always so easy to excel because while you were taught how to *do* what you do, rarely are you taught how to *market* or *sell* what you do. That causes you to begin to overthink how you should do it. And there are so many things to do that you get overwhelmed with doing all of it now.

For that part of your business, we are the bridge between where you are in your business to the vision you have for your life. We take what you have as a vision and develop the plan to get you there. Then, using the right tactics, we work with you to direct your message to the potential clients of your dreams, and put you on the path to the life you envision. The first step is getting roadblocks out of your way that you have inadvertently put in your marketing path.

In this book, as with all our books, we are trying to help you get better at one of the hardest parts of your business—keeping the overwhelm and overthinking from taking over your mind and your life. You will get the basics here, that will make your job easier and for the rest you can come to us at www.HowToGetThereFaster.com. We'll remind you about that a bunch.

If you have questions about the content, please email us at Info@YuloffCreative.com and we will do our best to answer. Put "Overthinking and Overwhelmed Book Content Question" in your subject line.

If you would like to book us to speak to your business group, you can send an email to Info@YuloffCreative.com and put "Sharyn and Hank Speak to Our Group" in your subject line. We have limited days each year but love to educate small business owners on the latest in marketing, human resources, sales, and public speaking.

We are here to think for you, work for you, create for you, figure it all out, and hand it to you.

Let's get started.

Sharyn and Hank Yuloff
Your Small Business Coaches for the Overwhelmed Overthinkers

Want More Training?
What if it was FREE?

No More Business Binders

Getting You Focused for Your Success

The Small Business
BREAKTHROUGH
BOOTCAMP

Hank and Sharyn Yuloff
share their proven secrets on how to create your own successful marketing plan...
And they're in person to coach you.
And for YOU, it's FREE!

All the info and register for your free ticket at FreeMarketingSeminar.com

Seating is limited. YCMS reserves the right to cancel this offer at any time.

Introduction—How to Use This Book

First, thank you for purchasing and actually cracking the cover of *The Marketing Checklist 3*. That you have done the second part, begun reading, sets you apart from most small business owners who are too busy being too busy to work *on* their business.

Over more than the past decade as a small business coaching team, we know that there are two reasons that *the work* never gets done. The first is that you, the small business owner, are overwhelmed. You are responsible for everything. Even if you can delegate, you still must check the work and make sure it's done correctly. That takes a toll.

The other half of that equation is when you *do* get into action to improve your business, you are shown dozens of options. The challenge is that most people who want to sell you a product are salespeople. They think that their whizbang deal is great for every business. We spoke to a woman the day before we wrote this page who runs a pain management clinic. She had been *sold* online ads and other things that she never should have bought. They were poorly targeted and there were no options to change the messaging to suit her business. Then she had a web person who was trying to get her to rebuild her website. The part that made us sad is that as often as we see poorly built websites, hers was done well. Sure, there were some adjustments she could make, but this person wanted to charge her $3,500 which she did not have for an unneeded rebuild.

We see this every week. No wonder you are overwhelmed.

And when you are thrown all these options and supposed opportunities up against your proverbial marketing wall, you overthink which of them to use.

That's not productive or sustainable.

And, whether you invested $14.95 for the paperback or a few dollars for

1

the digital download, or you got this book for free from us, we want to give you help. Affordable help.

The reason? Well heck, you might know someone who is more overwhelmed and overthinking than you and when this book helps you improve your business, you might tell them about us. At the end of each chapter, we'll remind you how to do that.

Here is what else you will find at the end of each chapter: *Your action item.* We will give you information then we will tell you exactly how to implement that chapter to build your small business.

The book is divided into two parts. The first is more mindset related and the second is more nuts and bolts. We know what you're thinking as you read that last sentence. "Well, I can just jump ahead to the nuts and bolts. It will be faster." We will tell you—the reader—exactly what we would tell a coaching client: Do *not* jump over the mindset part to work on the nuts and bolts because "I just don't have the time." You overthinkers will need that first part before moving on. You see, what overwhelms you the most are the roadblocks that you put in your own way. (Every one of our coaching clients just began nodding their head and thinking, "Yep—they've gotten rid of some of those roadblocks for me." Yep—and you've just gone and added more.

We see you. We got you.

We suggest you open a new document on your computer or pull out paper and pen—*invest* some time to answer those action items. By doing that, you will be developing the basics of your marketing path. We say marketing *path* not marketing *plan* because a *plan* tends to get put on a shelf and becomes *shelf help.* Your marketing path will change. We promise you that it will. The best thing about being a small business owner is that you can be more flexible and take more rapid action.

Once you have this list, you will get to the end of the book, and we will give you more information on what to do. *No—don't go there now!* Goodness gracious, you overthinkers really are predictable. LOL, just trust the process. We got you.

Also, at the end of each chapter, we will offer the opportunity to give you thirty minutes of coaching time. If there is some action item that you just can't solve, book your time then. Otherwise, you may want to wait until you have finished the book and have more data; we can guide you through.

Here's just a bit more help: We do a lot of webinars that are free. When you want a schedule of those webinars, it is a page on our website which is at www.YuloffCreativeMarketingSolutions.com, but you can find it even faster at www.YourMarketingAdvisors.com.

One more important note: *Not one sentence in this book was written or researched by an artificial intelligence program.* Go ahead, ask us questions about the book—we will be able to answer them.

See you soon!

Sharyn and Hank

Part I

The Concept of Overthinking,
Being Overwhelmed, and
How to Improve Your Mindset to
Improve Your Sales and Marketing

Chapter 1

Your Warm-up! 10 Easy Marketing Tips

Welcome to our eighth business-building book. Before we jump into the deeper stuff, let's do a warm-up exercise. When you work out, they tell you to do some light stretching first to get your body ready. That's what this first chapter does; it gives you ten marketing tips to make your *mind* warm-up to building your marketing program. Some of these will be discussed in further detail later.

OK, take a deep breath, grab your highlighter, and let's jump in.

1. Optimize your website.
While you can certainly shell out money here, why not do it yourself? For the purposes of this book, please assume that *every time* we discuss your website, we are going to suggest that you build it, and *use* the WordPress program. All those cheap and theoretically easy-to-build sites that you see advertised generally do not give you the same bang for your buck (for SEO and everything else) as WordPress. Look at your search engine optimization and focus keywords and see how you can improve them. Ask your prospects what they typed into the Google machine to find you. Can you also improve your website's layout or content? Do you have a blog? If not, add one!

2. Create social media profiles.
Presence is a *big* deal for your small business, and you should be taking advantage of *all* the appropriate social media platforms out there. You never know where your next client will come from, and we get a consistent 12% of our new small business coaching clients from social media. Just make sure you are on the *right* platforms—those where your prospects are searching for you. Here is an example: We are small business coaches. We have a presence on Pinterest, but don't invest much time on the platform. Our favorite clients

are *not* searching for their business coach on that platform. We know this from testing.

3. Claim Google Business Profile.
Pretty self-explanatory. SEO is huge for getting your business found and your Google business listing (first called Google My Business) is *vital* since Google is the #1 search engine (as of this writing, anyway). We see lots of small businesses that use this as their pseudo web site, but we don't recommend that at all as anything more than a short-term fix while you build your website.

4. Build a referral network.
Networking is one of the most important things you can do. This is where *word of mouth* gets strengthened. You should always be looking to refer people that you know to people in need of the businesspeople that you know.

5. Blog regularly.
You want to be present, and you want to be active. Both are attractive to customers and blogging is a great way to tell your story to prospects. We discussed this in previous books, and webinars.

6. Ask for reviews.
Positive reviews are incredibly important for your business. When deciding between you and your competitors, your reviews and ratings are a differential maker. You should have a QR code that allows people to get right to the review section of your Google Business Profile. Put that QR code on a card that you carry with you. We even see people put them on their business card and have it say, "Check out our reviews!"

7. Answer online questions.
This one is a no-brainer. When someone calls you on the phone, you answer, so this is the same thing online. You'll get questions through Google and social media platforms. You want to respond as quickly as possible to all questions that are posted online regarding you, your business, and your services. Not answering might make you look like you don't know what you're doing, or even worse, that you are out of business.

8. Write thank you notes.
For reviews, purchases, blog feedback, etc. People love feeling like they're appreciated so let your customer base know that they matter! Here is the

system we currently use. It allows us to do the entire process online, but the recipient gets a real, printed card in the mail; one delivered by their postal person—YuloffCreative.com/Mailbox. Please note that if you use our system (system stands for *save yourself some time, energy, and money*) we make a few dollars, but you *do* get our help advice on using the system and what your cards should look like.

9. Spruce up your email signature.

A lot of people are guilty of this. If there's too much in your signature, it just annoys people; their eyes glaze over and they see none of it. You *must* have basic contact information here—phone and web address. You can add a slogan. We add one of our photos of the two of us and our Lucy (from *Peanuts*) photo—us with Lucy's yellow psychiatric booth but the signs say "The Marketing (or sometimes Business) Coaches are in." And "Marketing Help 5 C." Since this is a warm-up exercise, we won't go into the reason for this now.

10. Create a useful email newsletter.

Okay, let's be careful on how we define newsletter. Not everyone appreciates having their emails flooded and most hate email ads in general regardless of how infrequent they are. Our *newsletter* is a regular email that is a great way to keep our audience informed of what we're up to and keeps us at the forefront of their minds. So, create an email newsletter that features *free* advice. We include our next speaking gigs (if they are free) and tell them what they will learn. When we publish our blog, we let our audience know what it's about. Free. Free. Free. Serve. Serve. Serve their needs. Once a week is good, *not* more than that. At the least, your audience should hear from you monthly.

Your Action Item ❑

Which of these ten ideas are you going to implement first? We suggest you pick just one or two so you don't get overwhelmed. You can add more later.

* * *

If you have questions about this chapter or anything else you read in the book, you can book time with us at HowToGetThereFaster.com. It's your *free, get-your-business-focused call.* We'll mention it again. Thanks for investing in *The Marketing Checklist 3: Your Guide for Overwhelmed and Overthinking Entrepreneurs.* Let's keep going and get deeper.

That's the first chapter! We hope that you have already gotten your $14.95 worth!

Chapter 2

Do You Have the Mindset of the Technician That Saved Fed Ex?

Years ago, at the FedEx Memphis hub all the machines and conveyor belts *suddenly* stopped working. This was disastrous to the company for two reasons:

1. All FedEx packages at the time went to Memphis first and then were shipped out all over the world.
2. And, FedEx *guaranteed* that it would be there when you needed it the next day.

FedEx's reputation and millions of dollars were on the line. So, they called a technician to come in to see if he could fix it.

The technician came in and glanced at the facility, went to the center beam, and turned one screw a quarter turn. And like magic everything started working again.

Fed Ex founder (now CEO) Fred Smith was ecstatic and asked the technician, "What do I owe you?"

The technician said "$10,000."

Mr. Smith replied, "what $10,000? You were here for less than five minutes."

The technician said, "Yes, it's $10,000."

Smith, thinking he could out fox the technician, asked, "May I see an itemized receipt?

"Sure, give me a napkin," said the technician and wrote on the napkin.

Fred Smith looked at the napkin, nodded his head and smiled, and went straight to his office safe and got him $10,000 in cash.

On the napkin it said, "Turning screw $1, knowing which screw to turn $9999."

If you're struggling to get more leads and more clients, our guess is that it's not a matter of you *working harder* . . . we're pretty sure you *do* work hard. It's simply a matter of spending your time turning the right screws . . . just a few degrees.

What are the activities that have the biggest impact in your business?

What are the skills and abilities (your *screws*) that once developed will give you the biggest return on the time invested.

One of those *screws* that will have a *major* impact in your life and business is the ability to influence people.

We can speak from personal experiences that the moment we started to *really* focus on increasing our ability to help small business owners—our lives changed forever.

Suddenly people were inviting us into to their inner circles. Sales situations that would make most coaches cringe, felt like conversations we'd have with a sibling. And, most importantly, we felt empowered to really create whatever life we desired.

Your Action Item ❏

What is *your* $10,000 screw? What two or three skills do you bring to the table that will make your prospect smile and write you a check?

* * *

If you are ready to experience this kind of shift in your life and your business, it could begin with a small conversation. There is no sales pitch, though we will give you a website to check out after our call. For your free 30-minute *get-your-business-focused call*, head to HowToGetThereFaster.com.

Chapter 3

Starting Your New Business ... or ... Catching What You Missed the First Time

Having worked with dozens of brand-new small business owners just like you, we know the most exciting *and* the most frightening question you will have to ask yourself before starting your business will come after you do an extensive search for competition and find that no one is in your area.

That question is, "Why isn't anyone doing this?"

Often, after a bit more research we have been able to answer that question with, "Oh, *that's* why."

In fact, we've had it happen to ourselves. We thought that opening a publishing house for only brand-new business book writers would be easy. Then we had our advisors ask us these questions:

- Have you worked with first time authors? (yes, as a matter of fact)
- If so, how many? (well . . . one)
- Are you ready to hand hold them? How did it work out that first time? (not very well)
- How much are you going to charge them for editing? (probably more than my editor charges me, since they're new)
- How are you going to handle publishing rights? (they will keep them)
- How are you going to handle *all* the money issues? (monthly payouts?)
- How are you going to handle re-orders on the distribution platform? (once a month order time)
- How long will your contract be with these authors? (a year, with automatic renewals?)
- What if you don't like working with some of them? Do you have an

out in your contract? (well, we do *now*!)
- Can they publish them outside your publishing house? (of course, but they will no longer be part of our seminar team)
- Since all the names of the books are going to be similar (Did I tell you? It was a series and they all started with the same three words.), what happens if an author removes their title from the series? Can they re-title it?
- What if, during the writing and editing process, the author becomes too difficult to work with? (As Sharyn says, slow to hire, quick to fire.)

That kept going for about forty other "what if" and "are you kidding" questions. It should be obvious by now that we decided that our Naked Book Publishing company was going to be reserved for our books only.

This exercise of starting a new business, even though it was a division within our current business and would support our core private small business coaching business, reminded us that you should always check with those who have gone before you prior to taking that costly leap. It is what we have taught all our small business private coaching clients when they have a really cool idea and ask, "What do you guys think?"

In fact, if we don't have experience with what a client needs, we go out and get that information instead of guessing. Guessing can be costly in both time and money. So are hunches. And your gut.

It isn't that there aren't tons of incredible ideas to be thought. But we want to avoid becoming part of that statistic. You know the one—that a very high percentage of small businesses do not make it past the first couple of years.

Let me give you another personal story that led us to go through the exercise I just described to you. *What Adam Ace did for me:*

We used to be part of a mastermind group that met twice a year. It was all business owners and several of us were asked to teach different sections of the breakouts. During one breakout where we were not teaching, I saw that Adam Ace was teaching and I was excited to go see what he had to share. Adam is by trade a comedian (three-time College Comedian of the Year) but has a good head for business.

When I walked into his session, I was amazed to be the only one in the room. Clearly everyone figured incorrectly that Adam was *just* a comic. When he saw me, he said, "I am glad you came in . . . I have been watching what you and Sharyn are doing and I cannot figure out your focus. Lay it out for me."

At the time, we *were* lacking focus. We were business coaches first, but *also* had a promotional product company, and offered a cool appreciation tool through www.YuloffCreative.com/mailbox, (which we use every week). *And* we had the idea that we were going to turn the publishing company that we had created for our own books (Naked Book Publishing, "Business Stripped to the Basics") into a place where business book writers had a place to promote and sell their books. *And*, that would lead to speaking opportunities for all of us as we would create small business seminars around the country. *And*, there were also a couple of online product ideas.

Yeah . . . it was a lot.

Even as I was sketching it all out, I could see that all these projects were keeping us from focusing completely on the success we wanted to achieve for our business and our small business owning clients.

It took twenty minutes, and I laid it all out for Adam. It was quite the flow chart. He patiently listened to all of it, then he paused and shared some words of wisdom that resonates with me years later. I share them with you now in case you are challenged with the same affliction as an entrepreneur.

"Hank," he said, "I appreciate that you are an entrepreneur. I applaud it. Truly. But . . . just because you think something would make a good business, does not mean you have to be the one to create it."

Ouch. Double ouch.

And I am going to pause here just in case you just had a *come-to-your-creator* moment as I did.

But Adam was right. It was time to put almost everything on the back burner, or back in the freezer. Especially Naked Book Publishing. The concept of putting on seminars with lots of business experts seemed like a lot of fun, but it was not going to help us achieve our goals. It was mostly going to help them reach *their* goals without an appropriate amount of profit for the work we were going to have to put in. In fact, as we looked at it, the choice was the publishing company or our private small business coaching practice. We had reached an important moment and needed to make a decision.

The compromise was that we only help our coaching clients with their books and guide them through their own publishing journey.

We still offer promotional products, but they are not what we highlight in a networking situation. We still offer the appreciation tool, but mostly for the use of our clients. Well, and you, of course if you click that link.

The moral of the story is that now, each time one of us . . . ok . . . *me* . . . comes up with an idea or hears something and says, "That would be a great business idea," Sharyn smiles, looks at me, and says, *"just because."*

That gets us instantly focused, I hope it does the same for you.

Your Action Item ❏

Layout the steps you have taken and the steps you still need to take as you launch your small business. This could also be your new idea inside your currently running business. Put them in the order of which item needs to be done first through the last.

* * *

Let us help. If you found this chapter to be highly interesting, we know you are probably looking to begin your successful business with a plan. As you take your first steps, your path now has many possible directions. How do you focus and decide on the best one to take? That's what we as small business coaches do for folks just like you. Wouldn't it be great if your marketing, sales and human resources could be much easier? It's time! Press *your* easy button! We work for you, think for you, create for you, and figure it all out. Let's have a conversation about it by going to www.HowToGetThereFaster.com.

Chapter 4

Starting Your New Business ... or ... Catching What You Missed the First Time— The Sequel

In the last chapter, we shared a story of how we had a great idea for a business that was going to support our core business and how after doing lots of due diligence, we decided that it was not such a great idea. That chapter is giving your heart it's due. This chapter is now talking to your brain.

We want to help you go through that decision-making process. Let's begin to discuss how to test whether your idea is viable, how to vet your idea, and how to decide if there is a market for your idea.

With the internet, it has become a much easier task than in decades past to check for the potential viability of your idea. When we have a client who is starting her new business, we do a Google search using several different phrases that her ideal client might type in to find her. Let's use our ill-fated publishing company as an example.

We did a search and did not find that anyone was indeed doing what we wanted to do. There *were* lots of people who coached new authors through the process, but we didn't find where someone was bringing them all together in one place.

We found this out by doing some research into our idea. Then, we did several searches with phrases like this: "First-time business authors." "New business authors." "Coaching for first time business authors." "Publishing company for new business authors." "How much does it cost to start a publishing company."

That last one was very important: let's get to that one in a moment. If you have done an exhaustive search and you are not dissuaded, that is great. Before you move on, do another search. This search will be the least expensive part of your new business and can save you lots of heart ache.

I know; I am such a downer. Sorry, but as your small business coaches, we want you focused and prepared for everything that will come next.

Now let's move on to the money.

Two of the most important questions you must answer when we talk about your new business are "How are you going to pay for it?" And, "How are you going to get paid?" Let's go with the first one first.

There are a lot of things you must budget for when planning to start your own small business. Here are a few questions that you need to answer:

- How are you going to plan and budget for short- and long-term costs, like taxes, fees, subcontractors, employees, equipment, and rent?
- How are you going to budget for all the hidden fees most don't expect? These include insurance, incorporation, and administrative costs. And don't forget legal. We have found that using a service like Legal Shield helps on that last one and added our affiliate link to the blog.
- It is all going to boil down to two big questions: How much should you plan to save before starting a business? And should you try to accumulate a surplus fund in case things go wrong?

Those last two questions are going to lead to a couple more that most entrepreneurs ignore: Do you have enough money to cover your costs for an extended period of time while you ramp up? If your first reaction when you read that question was, "how long is extended?" give yourself a star. But you are not going to like the answer. Plan for a year. You must go through an entire yearly cycle to see if your idea is going to be proven. And if your year was like 2020, then double it.

If you have gotten past the dollars part of your plan, then we can move on to writing the business plan phase, which brings us back to that second question about money—how are you going to get paid?

To answer that question, you must answer these questions:

- What are you selling? The more specific you can get the better. For example, we do not say we sell coaching services. We narrow it down to "we are the virtual marketing department for successful small business owners who are so busy doing what they do, they do not have time to properly market what they do." As a bonus to marketing, we solve their human resources, sales, and public speaking challenges with a combination of online, technical, and traditional marketing tactics.
- Who are you selling it to? This is going to take a long time to answer. The hint is that the word *everyone* is not the correct one. We have

several webinars online that talk about how you find and target your niche.

- How much are you selling it for? The quick answer, you are probably asking too little.
- How will they pay you? There are lot of options: checks, credit cards, and a variety of online options exist. Decide on the one that costs you the least compared to what it does for you.

We just created a webinar for small business owners who have a new idea or have a new business. Here is our table of contents of the seventeen things that you are going to have to create.

Create Your Team

You are going to need your Board of Advisors. This could be official or not. Here are some of your important teammates:

- Your banker from a small locally-based institution would be great.
- Your accountant and your financial advisor to go through your numbers and decide what kind of entity you should be using.
- Your chief marketing officer to create your path, create and define your brand, and bring in sales (we volunteer for this job!).
- A graphic artist to create your logo and keep your look or brand consistent in all your outward facing publication points.
- Who you choose to develop your website is very important. We have come across far too many who know how to code in WordPress but have no concept of how to make your website work correctly from a business point of view. We got so tired of fixing client's sites that we created a free tool you can use. It's at www.ThisWebsiteUnderConstruction.com. It will walk you through things you need on your site. By the way, since you are now a new or better marketer, we will share this *inside information* with you. We use that site as a sales funnel for business owners to find us. We make it very clear on the site: If you need a website, you probably need business coaching as well.
- Your business lawyer can keep you from getting into trouble. You may want someone local, but we also like the services that Legal Shield provides (we are affiliates for Legal Shield and think that for $40 a month it is going to save you thousands of dollars a year).
- You need a local print shop.
- You also need an information technology person to keep your computers running well.

We have had clients and potential clients on our board as well as business owners that we respect. And don't forget your mom!

Business Entity
There are several ways you can set up your business, each with their own advantages and disadvantages as well. Your lawyer, accountant, and financial planner will help you decide between a sole proprietorship, Limited Liability Corporation (LLC), an S or C type corporation or some variation of a partnership. Tax considerations will very much come into play with your entity.

How Will You Get Paid?
If you have a business, someone is going to have to pay you for your products or your services. There are lots of electronic methods (Venmo, Paypal, credit card portals) as well as the tried-and-true checks and cash. Compare the cost of each of these compared to the convenience they offer.

Who Are You Marketing To?
Marketing is a science of choice. It helps people predisposed to buying your product know that you are there for them. This is one of the most important of my statements for coaching businesses. You never create your marketing messages without knowing exactly who you are creating it for.

Who Is Your Customer?
Most small business owners have between three and six different categories of clients. Name them and break each of them down by the demographics and psychographics. Know that you will need different messages for each different category. It is *vital* that you invest the time it takes to narrow down the niches you will be marketing to with every marketing tactic.

Your Budget
You always must come up with the answer to the question that your investors and your bank will be asking: How are you going to pay for it? Each industry has its own numbers, but the range of the operating budget for start-ups will be between 11 and 20% of expected revenue.

Naming Your Idea
Prior to opening you are going to have to name your company. Always check to make sure you own the name of your company as a URL. For most small businesses the owner of the company, most likely you, will be the brand of the

company. In addition to the name of your company, you need to own yours. You should also own the most common misspellings of your name. It's why we own UloffCreative.com in addition to all the proper spellings. You should also check for these names on the social media platforms you are going to use to connect with your clients as well as on the URLs.

Where to Find Your Clients

It is rather obvious that you must be able to find your target market members. It is a critical part of growing your business. If you cannot list numerous ways to reach your target market to generate sales, then you have probably not chosen a specific enough market, or it is a demographic that is not easily accessible, or you have not called Yuloff Creative yet for your free marketing consultation.

It is vital that you be able to reach them. If you can't find them, you can't deliver your message to them. What that means for you is that you will not be able to generate awareness, which ultimately means you will not be able to get them on your list and convert them into paying clients.

Here are some examples of where you can find them:
- Chamber of commerce meetings (virtual or in person)
- Trade shows and conferences: either attending or exhibiting or speaking
- Direct mail to a mailing list of potential clients
- Websites or blogs they visit
- Advertising in periodicals, journals, or newsletters that they read
- Social media groups
- Social media platforms
- Podcasts they listen to
- Related products and services they buy
- Speaking to various clubs and organizations
- Teaching a webinar
- Ad or article in their newsletter
- Advertise on their website

How to Sell Your Idea

You can sell your services in three ways. You can focus on price, speed of delivery of service, or quality of product and service. You can only offer any two of the three, not all of them . . . unless you wish your business to die an untimely death.

Implementing Your Sales

We want you to remember something very important: You are not in the (fill-in-the-blank) business, you are in the business of marketing your business. Using the proper sales funnels will make that easier. We have included a mock-up of your sales funnel and how ours look.

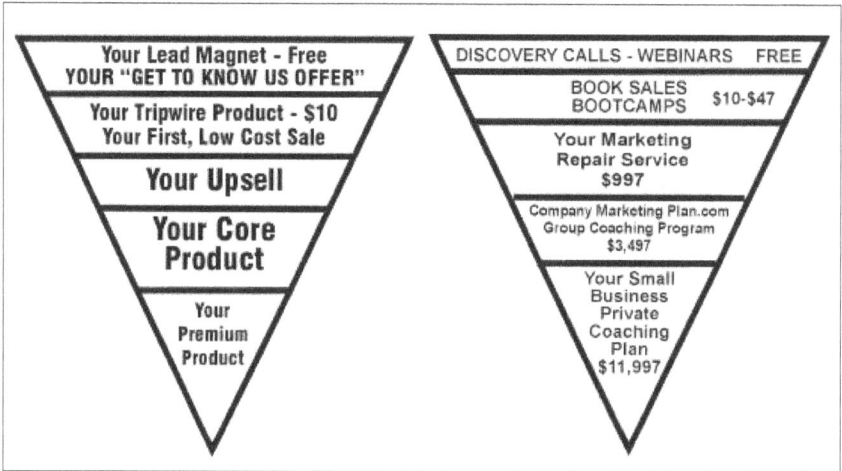

Your Logo

You will need a logo as a representation of your company. Here are a few tips: Keep it simple. The colors you choose matter as do the typefaces. Keep it easy to read and for goodness sakes, don't do it yourself. Marketing tip: Have a vertical and a horizontal version of your logo. That way you can use them in different places.

Your Website

People look for every service on the internet (it used to be the *Yellow Pages*). Your website is far more than a brochure and must be kept constantly relevant as it tells your story. Your website will be the hub of your online presence. It is where your clients will be invited to learn about your business. It is where you can enroll people onto your list in exchange for your lead magnet.

It is important to remember that your website standing alone will *not* generate new clients or sales unless you drive traffic to it. Once you have them there, you must have a well-designed conversion process waiting for them.

You should make sure it is built in WordPress as that is the most favored program by search engines.

If your website is under construction, *put it at the top of your to do list* and commit to getting it done.

Here is a brief website checklist:

- When your target audience arrives, will it represent you, your brand and what you are selling?
- Do you have the basic pages—home, service, about, testimonials, blog, contact?
- Does your copy speak to your audience and what they are looking for?
- Do you have video testimonials? Do you have appropriate testimonials on each page that match the content?
- Is your phone number on the upper right-hand corner?
- Is your website adaptive and responsive?
- Do you have an opt-in offer?
- Does your page tell your story?
- Do you have professionally shot photos and welcome video?

If you want help creating your website our free tool for building websites is at www.ThisWebsiteUnderConstruction.com.

Your Social Media

Treat your social media like any other marketing tactic. It is not the silver bullet for success and how you use it depends on your marketing goals. Use social media for communicating with clients, to develop new business, to share business tips, and to be a trusted referral source.

Your Video

You will be able to use video on every platform you use for your marketing—website, social media, blogs, email, your video products. It is the most effective way to share your marketing message.

How To Follow Up

The saying that your fortune is in your follow up is entirely true. Here is the odd challenge to go with that saying: Only 10% of sales people make more than three contacts. And 80% of sales are made on the fifth to twelfth contact. You *must* implement a consistent follow-up system to make your contacts the most effective. We have entire blogs and videos on follow up for you to reference.

Speaking to Your Audience

Using your voice is incredibly important. We use several different methods to share our message from stages of all sizes. We run our own seminars. We are always available to speak on panels on various marketing subjects. We have MCed other events and been keynote speakers. We also love to host our own webinars.

Appreciation Program

In the words of Kody Bateman, "Appreciation wins out over self-promotion every single time. A system for letting clients and potential clients know you are thankful for their time, consideration, and their business is important.

Let's End with Some Rules of the Road

Here are a few general rules of the road that you need to follow:

- You will never use the term *"I just needed something done fast. I will go back and do it right later."* We have seen it. You won't. Do it right the first time.
- You will never use the term "Eh . . . it's good enough." How you do one thing is how you do everything. Do it as well as you can every time.
- You will never be caught saying, "Oh, I can't do that," or "but I don't have the time," or "I'm just a little business."
- You will never use the term, "Let's just get started and we'll fix it later."

Your Action Item ❏

Start sketching out your answers to all the different points in this chapter. It's going to take a bit of time. Then, when you are stuck or feel that you are overwhelmed, head to HowToGetThereFaster.com and book your 30-minute *get-focused* call. We will move you forward to your next steps.

* * *

If these last two chapters spoke to you, we know you are looking to begin your successful small business with a plan. As you've taken your first steps, your path now has many possible directions. How do you focus and decide on the best one to take? That's what we do for you and hundreds of other small business. Wouldn't it be great if your marketing, sales, and human resources could be much easier? It's time! Press *your* easy button! We work for you, think for you, create for you, and figure it all out and hand it to you.

Chapter 5

12 Effective Management Principles

We hear it from virtually every prospect we talk to about coaching their small business, "I am so busy, I don't have time for (fill in the blank—marketing, sales, hiring someone, networking, etc.)." At that point we shift the conversation to how they are using their time.

It really is true that we all have the same twenty-four hours in a day.

So, let's make this a quick chapter on ways you can get more done.

1. Determine what is urgent. Here's another way of thinking about this one: What thing on your *to do* list will put cash in your pocket fastest?

2. Don't over commit. We had a business coach who taught us a very important lesson. The power of the word *no*. "No, I don't want to serve on that committee." "No, I don't want to go to dinner on Saturday." "No, I don't want to go have a beer, I'd rather spend time with my kid."

3. Have a plan for your time.

4. Always allow time for the unexpected! When it comes to almost everything, the amount of time it takes quite often is more than you blocked out. Heck, we added a full month onto the schedule of each of our books, so we hit our publish date.

5. Handle things once. This is *hard*! It will take practice.

6. Create realistic deadlines.

7. Set goals for yourself and your time.

8. Develop routines.

9. Focus on one thing at a time. Multi-tasking is, by and large, a croc. About the only multi-tasking we do is watch television while we work on some project on our laptops. This book? The content was sorted, given its first edit, and prepared to be sent to our editor, Terri

Boekhoff, while re-watching the *Will & Grace* series. (Thanks, Terri!)

10. Eliminate or minimize distractions. Having a cat in her lap is no longer a huge distraction for Sharyn.

11. Outsource tasks or delegate. If it costs less than $100 an hour, we have someone else do it. It all began with filing. Though we are mostly paperless now, I used to pay someone double the minimum wage to come over on a Saturday and file all the paperwork that goes along with our promotional product business. *Worth it!*

12. Leave time for fun and play. We *love* date night! Baseball games, movies, going to visit family is always worth it. Regenerate your mental and physical batteries.

Your Action Item ❏

Of the two authors on the front cover of this book, Sharyn is the best by far at managing time. Your job after this chapter is to look at your workflow and figure out where the two or three biggest time sucks are in your day.

* * *

It could be you need an organizer for your office or a virtual assistant to take some tasks off your list. We can connect you with proven, great people for both. Reach out to us through HowToGetThereFaster.com and we can talk about it.

Chapter 6

Getting Paid What You're Worth— 5 Rules of Pricing

When I was talking to my very first prospect, she asked me how much I charged. This was the first time I got near giving a price to anyone and I shared a number. The prospect asked me where I got my number. I told her that I had looked throughout my industry and I was pretty much average. Her answer to me was, "Oh, so your service is only average?"

It had never occurred to me to price our coaching based on researching the industry as a whole. Truth be told, the pricing came from very different research and pricing mistakes.

The very first time I created a marketing program, it was based on a bonus offered to promotional product clients—an affordable add-on sale with several deliverables. It was way underpriced, and few bought it. I ran it past a coach who solved that challenge. "Double it."

My thought was, "What the heck, let's try it." I did. And sales went up.

Since the subject of pricing for services came up during two private coaching calls this week, as well as during our Monday mastermind call, the universe must be asking me to share thoughts here, too.

First rule of pricing in getting paid what you are worth: You deserve to make a fair profit.

This is a *huge* bit of mindset magic. Remind yourself this each time you are tempted to give a lower price just to get the business. I will share with you that each time we have done this, it has been a mistake.

Second rule of pricing in getting paid what you are worth: There is a good possibility that you are not charging enough. This is a conversation you are having with your subconscious. If you are not charging an appropriate amount, your subconscious is already letting you know about it. If you listen closely, you will hear it. It might be in the form of resentment for having to work your tail off for too little money.

Third rule of pricing in getting paid what you are worth: Rather than cutting your prices, you may want to have tiered pricing for a tiered level of services. The Sears and Roebuck Company introduced a pricing structure that served them well. It is the "good, better, best structure." Human nature will have most of us choose the middle option because we don't want to pay the most, but we don't want the worst version, either.

In our coaching program we use a tiered, "good, amazing, freakin' amazing structure."

The "good" is our online program. You go to YourMarketingAdvisor.com, find all our free online webinars for the month and show up. Since we can do several a month, that's a bunch of hours of training a month. You can get a lot of general marketing help.

For the next two levels, we created the coaching programs we looked for, thought we had found, paid a lot of money for, and were disappointed with every time.

The "amazing" is our group coaching program—The Small Business Marketing Plan. We have put all our best video trainings into a marketing vault, with three full length Small Business Breakthrough Bootcamps *including* the *action* guide that allows you to put together a pretty nifty marketing plan. The best part of this is that you get several hours of two-on-you private coaching with us and you get to join our Monday mastermind video calls. To check this program out, go to www.CompanyMarketingPlan.com.

The "freakin' amazing program" includes the Small Business Marketing Plan *plus* you get weekly two-on-you coaching time along with dozens of other deliverables including writing blogs, elevator pitches, and emails for you. We create or correct your slides for presentations. And lots more, including dealing with your human resources challenges. We look at this program as being the hand-holding, safety net for small business owners.

Fourth rule of pricing in getting paid what you are worth: The concept of "the value-add" bonus. Most small business owners we talk to struggle with what to do when a prospect asks for a discount. They seem to always get asked about lowering their costs. We think that offering a bonus for clients as an add-on for services is a better value compared to a price drop. You should look for something that is worth a lot to your client but does not seriously affect your bottom line. By the way, giving away more time *does* seriously affect your bottom line because part of getting paid what you are worth includes having more of your time to do what you want to do.

For both of our coaching programs, we decided that a thirty-day money back guarantee would be the best value-add for us and our clients. We tested it for a year and decided that it worked well so we kept it on the program. It turns out that we never saw other coaches who were or are willing to give a money back guarantee.

Fifth rule of pricing in getting paid what you are worth: Don't be afraid to test. Pricing can be an educated guess at first. Unless you have a magic mirror on the wall, there is a bit of guessing. Your key to doing less guessing is to do enough research to minimize the guesswork. Here is one mistake that most new entrepreneurs make: You will be tempted to under charge to gain a share of the market. Or you will tell yourself that you want to build a track record of good service so you can raise your prices. When this thought creeps in your subconscious will now remind you of rule number one and if you are serious about getting paid what you are worth, you won't treat yourself as a beginner.

Your Action Item ❏
Take a close and honest look at what you are charging for your services. Ask yourself if you are getting paid what you are worth.

* * *

To discuss whether you are getting paid what you are worth, or your pricing or anything else in your marketing, we would like to offer you a *free marketing consultation*. Let's begin our conversation by increasing your profits by setting your rates at the right levels. Go now to www.HowToGetThereFaster.com, answer a few quick questions that will get us ready to speak to you, and you can choose a time in our calendar.

Chapter 7

Can You Do It for Less?
I'll Be Your Best Customer

From the very beginning of this chapter, we would like to explain that it is our overriding belief that as an entrepreneur, you absolutely, positively deserve to earn a fair profit for the excellence you bring to the table for your clients. Even though you are the best at what you do, at some point a prospect will ask you to lower your rates or provide a discount of some kind.

If you have been to our Small Business Breakthrough Bootcamp, you have heard Hank's story about the two brothers who own an auto parts rebuilding company that were a promotional product client. They were nice guys, but made it impossible for him to make a profit because each time he brought them a promotional product marketing idea, their comment was, "Yes, but what is *our* price?" They were also a client that he had to chase for payment, which lowered his profit even more. That's because there is a rule called the "value of money over time." The longer it takes for you to collect a past-due invoice, the less your money collected is worth because you did not have it in your business working for you. Hank finally gave them the business card of a competitor that they should use for their promotional products and stopped calling on them. The time spent, plus the discounts required, taught Hank that there are some kinds of business we should not go after. You cannot be everything to every client if you want to stay in business. We have used that same rule in our small business coaching programs.

Still, as many companies tighten their budgets during lean times, you may begin to receive discount requests more often. Whether you choose to work with a customer's pricing requests or stand firm on your pricing, you should always have a few responses ready. *Here, we* share seven powerful replies to use when you hear the words, "It costs too much."

1. *"Good question. Do you see price being your major obstacle to our deal?"* Sometimes, prospects just want to know whether you will consider reducing your prices. If they can't get a lower price, they will move on. Other times, they may be okay paying your rate but interested in receiving a discount if they can. By asking this question, you help determine their motivation.

2. *"We can definitely have a conversation about specific numbers, but let's make sure we're on the same page about this solution being a good fit for your needs."* With this response, you don't take a discount off the table, but you remind the prospect that it's not relevant until you're both sure it's a good fit. If you grant their request too soon, you will seem overly eager to close, which will work against you during the actual negotiation.

3. *"Why?"* Buyers sometimes haggle just for the sake of it. Oftentimes, those who say they are "just wondering" will pay your full price. It's important to understand where your prospect is coming from and customize the value exchange.

4. *"I can offer you a discount if we (extend the contract, adjust the terms of payment, go with X package or tier, register Y seats)."* Both parties should be prepared to compromise in a negotiation. If your customer or prospect asks for a discount, consider non-monetary requests that allow you to open the negotiating possibilities beyond price. Have you noticed that your cell phone companies offer you specials, but you must extend the term of your contract, usually by two more years?

5. *"What would you consider a reasonable discount?"* This question allows you to discern whether your customer or prospect can afford your product, or that they're not sold on the full value. If they don't have the budget for your solution, offer a less expensive or less comprehensive option. We have four different coaching programs, so that a prospect can chose their own discount but understand that it comes with a lower level of service. The service you will offer is still incredible, it is just with less time, or features.

6. *"What would need to happen to make our offering worth the price you were quoted?"* This question is a smart way to uncover gaps in your conversation and identify objections that may still exist. It's a chance to add or argue value for your solution and to earn full price if you meet the prospect's needs.

7. *"What if we connect next quarter? Do you think you'd have more budget open then?"* If your prospect is truly enthusiastic about working with you but simply doesn't have the budget, consider leaving them in your sales funnel, and continue to follow up with them in the future. We have found that this can sometimes be the best option for our business and the prospect. You may want to do what we have done and add into your offerings that you do not want them to buy if it is a financial hardship. It makes for a stronger long-term relationship, which, after all, is what you are after.

Bonus tip: Value added bonuses are a much better way to satisfy a prospect that is intent on slashing your bottom line. Find the thing you can offer as a value-added bonus rather than succumb to discounting. We can show you how to do that using content you already have, or easily can, create.

Everybody wants a deal. In a tight market, you may be tempted to give in to the discount request from prospects. The smarter move, though, is to have some responses ready when your customers ask for a deal. By doing so, you position yourself as a true value provider rather than selling yourself short.

Your Action Item ❑

Write down your answers to the questions in this chapter. There will be times when you must decide to walk away from a sale. Whether it is a potential client or someone you are working with, your peace of mind and your balance sheet deserve to both be positive. When that is a challenge that you are facing, remember this chapter and that you were given permission to move on to the next prospect who will respect what you do and appreciate what you do for them.

* * *

If you want help finding your line—your point of no return, connect with us at HowToGetThereFaster.com for your 30-minute *"setting your best pricing rules"* and we will talk about how to properly set your sales parameters to ensure you still make the profit you deserve.

Chapter 8

Help! I'm an Introvert Stuck in an Extrovert's Body!

Are you an introvert stuck in an extrovert's body? As a board member for several chambers, I have been part of organizing networking events for different business communities for decades. I find that for many of us, networking doesn't come naturally, instead it gives way to lots of social anxiety.

The truth is that networking events offer you, the hard-working business leader, the opportunity to make new connections outside of your areas of expertise and make new relationships within your industry.

Here are actionable tips you can take that will allow you to plan for, engage, and maintain relationships from networking events. I realize that it's not as easy as it sounds, however if you give these experienced-based tips a shot, it will give you the tools to further your professional relationships.

Are you ready to make your business networking more effective?

Having been to hundreds of networking events over the years, I can attest to the fact (as I am sure many can) that networking can sometimes be an awkward, uncomfortable, and clunky task for any business professional. Given the opportunity, many introverts like me (actually, I am an outgoing introvert) would stand off to the side and have a running mental commentary about what everyone else was doing. I have learned over time though, that you can build great business relationships if you put yourself in the right mindset, set proper goals, and be engaged in the opportunity.

If you are an introvert stuck in an extrovert's body, here are several tips to keep in mind at your next networking event.

Call a Friend
Before you go, call a friend. If you are a bit shy, having a friend to go to the event with can help. Go in with the game plan that you are not going to just talk to *each other*. You *must* both engage other people, bring them into your little circle of two, and expand it.

Networking Event Goals

What is your goal for your networking meeting? In sports, we call it having your game plan. Before a baseball game, our pitchers and catchers would go over the scouting report for the other team's hitters and plan for the types of pitches and locations we would pitch to them. To help you create your game plan do these things: Look at the website of the host and sponsors to figure out who you want to thank for hosting. Then look at the registration list (if it is available) and target specific contacts or specific job titles so you can be on the lookout for them. I have been known to send an email in advance saying "*Wow!* I see you are attending too. Let's make a point to connect and chat about your new (some service I learned about on their website)."

Conversation—What Do I Talk About?

If you are not the best at beginning conversations, hang around the food and beverages area. There will be a constant stream of people coming by and you can have something instant in common, "Oh my god, you like potato chips, too? Wow! Say . . . what do you do when you are not piling your plate full of cocktail weenies?"

Let's take a moment to talk about what you're going to talk about—you know, small talk. Small talk is kind of a big deal. Studies show it makes up about one-third of all adult human speech. Whether you're chatting about the weather or last night's game, these light conversations matter more than you think.

We've heard experts say that healthy relationships are never all business. Before you can establish deep trust with anyone—colleagues, clients, prospects—you first need to get to know them. And the laid-back sunny conversation involved in small talk is a great way to get to know people. The more people get to know you, the more comfortable they feel and the more likely they are to want to collaborate with you.

Engaging in small talk can also help boost your mood. Social relationships are not sufficient in themselves to generate new business, but they are an essential ingredient in relationship building.

So, how can you improve the important social skills of small talk? Here are four steps:

1. Have a plan. (We keep coming back to plans, don't we?) If you know you are attending an industry event or after-work gathering, prepare for it. Think about what you could discuss when meeting someone new. How could you help put the other person at ease? Would

you share any potential commonalities with them? It's important to determine the goal of casual conversations. This can help take some of the stress out of small-talk situations.

1. Turn your discomfort outward. Maybe your palms get sweaty, or your heart starts to race when talking with people you don't know. You might worry about talking too much or not enough. Or maybe the other person brings up a topic you don't know much about. Instead of dwelling on these feelings of anxiety, we suggest turning your discomfort outward. Small talk can potentially expand your world, while dwelling on yourself shrinks your world.

2. Arrive with a set of questions. You don't necessarily need to pull up a list on your phone but run through some questions in your head. I will admit to you that I have used a 4x6 card in my jacket pocket with reminders. One of our favorite questions is to ask the other person what they do and how they got interested in that line of work. *And* as a follow up, "I bet six-year-old (first name) had something else planned." Or you could ask the other person where they live and what their hometown was like. From where they live, it's a short pivot to talk about vacation destinations, so you could also ask them about a favorite place they have visited or somewhere they'd like to travel.

3. Share about yourself. Small talk should involve all parties. If you're only asking questions but never revealing anything about yourself, you may come off as nosy or intrusive. A good rule of thumb is to share about as much as the other person. You can also give yourself an exit strategy, by saying something like, "Great to meet you! Please excuse me. I'd like to greet some other people while I'm here."

What might seem like polite chitchat before a meeting or at an event can be incredibly useful at building rapport and establishing meaningful relationships. If you tend to feel uncomfortable with small talk or want to get better at chatting with others in small amounts of time, consider applying some of the tips above.

Elevator Pitch
Here is our favorite two-sentence elevator pitch format. You will be polished without looking like you practiced in front of your mirror for an hour:

> You know how (*your audience*) struggles with
> (*the shortest way to explain the problem you solve*)?
> Well, I make it so that they (how they feel after they work with you).

> Here's an example from our business using that format:
> You know how most business owners really struggle
> with knowing how to market online? Or off?
> Well, we hold their hand when they go interneting for new business.

That was twenty-eight words, and I made up the phrase "interneting for new business" as a way that they hunt for sales. But you got the point. And that's what matters, right? You could wake us up out of a sound sleep and ask what we do, and those words would probably come babbling out.

Here's a supersecret ninja networking tip: Your pitch should be no longer than thirty-two words.

Interest—Be a "Ted" Instead of Being a "Ting"

Instead of worrying about being the most interes*ting* person in the room by trying hard to come up with quips or anecdotes, be Interes*ted* in what the people you meet are sharing. When you're open to listening to the other person and asking follow-up questions like "tell me more about . . ." and "how did you decide on . . ." you are remembered as a great conversationalist with very little effort on your end. This takes the pressure off you, helps you learn more about your contact, and helps them remember you as being a great listener. It also may turn them into a prospect!

If You're a Supreme Introvert, Get Involved

Getting involved in an organization, joining committees, or taking board positions can help you develop very strong relationships and bring great dividends. You will gain greater visibility and can be seen as a resource to others, which allows you to talk about your business, eventually. *Also*, the work done for committees tends to be in small groups. As the band Supertramp sang, "Give a Little Bit." Remember that networking is a two-way street. Help others by introducing them to your connections, offering suggestions, or assisting them when needed. By offering your time to people, they will remember the favor and introduce you to others as a powerful resource.

Volunteer

There have been times where if I arrive early to an event I start helping with check in and make myself the unofficial greeter. I stand at the door, say hello, ask people what they do and then I ask, "who do you want to meet at this event?" If I meet that type of person, I instantly walk them over to the person who asked to meet them.

Ask for Introductions

It's okay to be the newbie! Go to the chapter admin, communications director, event planner, or the person that invited you to the event (typically listed on your registration confirmation) and ask them for introductions to those they think may be a good business fit. Their goal for these events are to connect people and keep you coming back, so be sure to use them as a resource. Here's your script: "Hey, I'm new. Who do I need to meet at this event?" They will ask you questions and based on your answers, you will get introductions.

Wrap It Up

If a conversation starts heading into uncomfortable topics, be sure to be respectful by politely excusing yourself to get a drink, food, use the bathroom, catch up with someone else, or make a phone call.

Thank You's and Follow Up's Go a Long Way

Trade shows and networking events have the same rule in our office: What good is gaining a contact if you don't keep in touch? After the event, we have twenty-four hours to reach out by phone, email, text, direct mail, social media, or some combination of all of them. We create an A list and a B list. The A list is critical to reach out to. Make sure that you connect with both lists on LinkedIn (if appropriate) and send a quick email as a "nice to meet you" or a follow-up on a conversation. If you promised to send something, let's get it in their hands *fast*. In our case, quite often it is one of our books on the topic we were discussing, or at least a special report (a two- or three-chapter e-book). It could also be a link to be a guest on our podcast, *The Marketing Checklist View Cast* (TheViewCast.com). Doing this within a twenty-four-hour window after the event will keep you top of mind and create a good base for future conversations and relationship development.

Oh, here's one more tip. It may not help you much, but it sure as heck helps us. A few years ago, we built a trade show booth based on the *Peanuts* character Lucy and her "Psychiatric Help" booth. It turns out, our target audience likes the booth and want to talk about the times in our lives when we used to read the comic strip. A technical term for the booth is a *Top of the Sales Funnel Attraction Piece*. If you want to talk about what would work for you get into our calendar.

Your Action Item ❏

When it comes to networking, we know that this is a challenge for most small business owners. The biggest challenge is that they want to get there faster. Create a list of three topics that you think you could talk about with almost anyone. They should have nothing to do with your business. Also, if you are an introvert, what extrovert are you going to channel when you go to an event? Check out their photo before you leave for the event. Fun, huh?

* * *

If you want to talk about this or any other "I'm an introvert stuck in an entrepreneur's body" issues, go to HowToGetThereFaster.com and we can work on your specific plan.

Chapter 9

Overthinking in Your Business: What Causes It

Every week (yes, including holidays) we hold a Monday mastermind call where all of our clients in the Group + Private coaching program and our private coaching program can jump on a video conference call and ask whatever question they want about their business. We get all sorts of issues and most of the time we handle them right there, and sometimes we must get back to them with an answer. Other members of the mastermind can give their thoughts as well. It's one of our favorite afternoons of the week because we are under no time constraints, and we get a lot done for our clients.

The most common thing that pops up is some challenge that the client needs help with to decide on the best ways to handle. Quite often the client could have handled it themselves, *but* . . . they spent so much time deciding on the right way to do it that they have become frozen instead of acting. We see it immediately.

They were overthinking it. Another way to visualize it is that they were putting roadblocks up in the path to their success. It wasn't put there by an outside force; it was them.

The causes of overthinking are varied. Here are eight that we regularly witness while working with clients:

- *Stress*—When you are stressed about something in your business, you are likely to spend a lot of time thinking about dealing with the situation and coming up with one, two, three or more possible answers. Then you must decide on the best one. And *is* it *really* the best one? This causes you to freeze in place.

- *Genetic Factors*—I had one therapist explain it to me this way: "Hank, it is literally all in your head and has been since pre-birth." Yes, it is possible to inherit the tendency of overthinking just like

41

other habits. Genetic factors can also predispose a person to excessive thinking, which may show up when the person is faced with difficult situations.

- *Illusion of Control*—This boils down to three words: Stuff's gonna happen. Your relationships, your finances, your health, and your future plans, we constantly want to control all the tiny details in life. In some areas we have very little control, but we do not realize it. This leads to overthinking, which presents itself as a strategy but is ineffective.

- *Need to be Certain*—This is the number one type of overthinking we see. People often try to know things with absolute certainty. For example, prospects for coaching want to know that we are indeed going to be able to help them. We can't guarantee it, mostly because we cannot control a client's actions. We only have control of *our* side of the equation. What we do, and it's what we teach our clients to do, is gather as many testimonials as they can about their business. This allows their (and our) prospects to have a greater certainty that they will succeed like hundreds of our clients have. This *is* an illusion of certainty in your mind, but it is impossible to be 100% certain. When we are in this situation, we give it our best shot and effort.

- *Striving for Perfection*—This is the second most common form of overthinking we witness. When you strive for perfection, it also leads to overthinking. There is a lot of focus on checking that everything is without flaw. This leads to a lot of time spent thinking and paying attention to detail. Gotta be honest here, when we were designing our Yuloff Creative logo, I had a file with over sixty possible images. Compare that to when I design a logo for a client, I can be *very* certain I did my best work with a small percentage of options. "The Great Yuloff Creative Logo Overthink" is a constant reminder to us that we, too, have been slaves to overthinking. It helps us coach better.

- *Avoiding Conflict*—Most people try to avoid any form of unpleasant-ness. To do this, we often play out scenarios in our heads as to how things may go and how to adjust our behavior.

- *Overgeneralizing the Effectiveness of Your Thinking*—When preparing for a client presentation, thinking can be very helpful. But we often apply the same technique to other situations, like how to market your business, it may be more of a hindrance than a solution. For example, thinking about what a competitor thinks about us.

- *Secondary Gain*—Thinking can have its indirect benefits too. Someone who overthinks may find themselves getting a lot of reassurance from family. It could also be a form of procrastination that delays unpleasant or difficult decisions or tasks. With our clients we see this mostly in the form of clients needing to create blogs or reacting with unknown people at a business event (like a chamber mixer).

We all do it to some extent (some more than others). Here are examples of clients demonstrating overthinking:
- "I have two social media posts for passing the two advanced architect exams. I'm not sure when to post them since I already have two posts that have gone out this week. When should I post these?"

- "I did my how-to-sell-your-business presentation to the networking group. There were two women from the same organization at the presentation who wanted the freebie and they put the same email. What should I do? I already sent one email before I saw it was the same."

- "Should I put an ad on golf course score cards?" (from a hypnotherapist that specializes in relationships)."

- "You know, it's very hard not to get discouraged when I have a bunch of prospects and none of them wants to do buy our CBD products."

- "Is it wrong for me to be pissed off when I sent out our meeting schedule with calendar invites to the entire sales department in June for all our meetings through October, and no one could make it to this last meeting because they didn't mark it down?"

- "What do you think about me getting another set of pens with our logo for our office in Oakland?"

- "What do you think is an acceptable number of phone calls to make in a day? What about a week? As we've worked on together, I dislike making calls, but I need to do it."

- "Yes, I need to focus. It seems like a double-edged sword. I don't think I can fit anything into my schedule because I am so busy. I acknowledge it isn't a good busy; it's chaotic and all over the place."

- These are all from incredible, successful businessmen and business-women. They work hard and once we show them the roadblock they constructed, they move ahead swiftly, implementing the solutions that became obvious once they took a breath, and we chatted for just a bit. What we did as their business coaches was the same as a pit crew for a race car driver; we gave them fuel to run on, made sure the air pressure in the tires was correct, and then pointed them in the right direction.

Your Action Item ❑

When it comes to overthinking . . . and *under*thinking, we know that this is a challenge for most small business owners. Recognize patterns in how you overthink. We see lots of clients that have what they call *problems* all the time, and they're the same type of problem. The way we teach them to look at these overthinking problems is as a roadblock, like you see on the streets of your town. Write down your roadblock pattern.

Now laugh at them and give yourself the grace to move forward. We all overthink. Let's keep it to a minimum.

* * *

And of course, if you can't recognize your methods, let's talk about it. We will take those blinders right off and get you on your path to success. How do you do that if I don't tell you how to connect with us? Let's have you read the next chapter on this topic first; the answer might just be there.

Chapter 10

Overthinking in Your Business: Ways to Halt the Irrational Desire to Overthink Everything

Roadblocks. There's nothing worse in business than having your goals delayed by that old saying, "Over-analysis leads to action paralysis."

"But" you may answer, "Slow progress is still progress."

Sure thing. But when you overthink everything, all the time, because you are setting expectations for yourself based on what you believe everyone else is doing or on what happens, that leads to nothing good. What's even worse is that most small business owners we witness that are overthinking are generally thinking that the worst outcome is likely to happen, and they sure don't want *that* outcome.

Here's the basic problem: The more you overthink, the less you do. So, get out of your head and get to it.

Here are ways to halt the irrational desire to overthink your decisions.

Recognize and Let Go of Perfectionism
Perfectionism is a roadblock to your making quick and effective business decisions since it's an exercise in all-or-nothing thinking. We recognize this with potential clients when they say, "If I am not ready to jump in 100%, then I just can't do it at all."

The latest person to give us that excuse a few months ago, just announced he was closing his staffing business. We were sad about his loss and for his employees who all must find a new job.

Another perfectionistic roadblock is the belief that if you make any choice other than the "correct" one, then you're a failure. That's an example of faulty thinking; it is the idea that there is only one right option.

Another way perfectionism can trip up your business is through the misconception that you have to know *everything*, anticipate each turn of events, and make a complete plan before acting. It's paralyzing to try to think through every potential way things could unfold.

You can fight perfectionistic tendencies by asking yourself these questions:

- Which of these choices would have the biggest positive effect on my top priorities?
- Of the people who will be aware of this decision, which one or two of them do I least want to disappoint?
- Are there actions I can take today that would move me towards realizing my goal?
- Given the information I have right now, what is the best thing to do next?

Focusing on your next step is much more realistic and beneficial than trying to anticipate what to do months or years in advance. We have found this to be a roadblock people use for procrastinating a decision. And that decision can cost you greatly.

Put Your Challenge in Perspective

Some decisions deserve lengthy and careful consideration, but many do not. Are you opening an office or retail location? It makes perfect sense to look and compare different neighborhoods and many locations within those neighborhoods. Prior to making your choice, take a written inventory of which priorities, people, and goals will be affected by the decision you make. That will clarify whether the choice at hand is meaningful, or of marginal importance.

The 10/10/10 test is a tool that works along similar lines. If you're worried about the consequences of a potential decision, ask yourself how you'll feel about it ten weeks later, ten months later, or ten years later. There's a good chance that the decision at hand will not be very important or even memorable in the larger scheme of things. By taking the long view, you can set aside your perfectionism and act toward your goal.

Here is another tool that we have found very useful. It's also much faster to implement. It's the 5/5 tool. "If it's not going to matter in five years, don't spend more than five minutes thinking about it."

If you're highlighting this book as you read, those last two paragraphs are definite highlights.

Here's a quote from Gary W. Keller that goes along with these tools, and you should ask yourself daily: "What's the one thing you can do today such that by doing it everything else will be easier or unnecessary?"

Let Your Intuition Take the Lead and Trust It

Intuition is a form of pattern recognition. When confronted with a business situation, your brain rapidly compares it to all your past knowledge and experiences, then offers you a *gut feeling* based on this initial assessment. This process is automatic and much faster than your conscious thoughts, so when time is of the essence and data in short supply, intuition can be the best way to make a choice. Studies have shown that the combination of intuition and logical thinking leads to faster, better, and more accurate decisions, and leaves you with more confidence in your decisions than you would have if you relied solely on analytical thinking. We discuss this in our webinars all the time. People tend to make decisions from an emotional point of view compared to a logical one.

It worked in Hank's life when he bought a car. He had been planning on purchasing a particular sporty vehicle—soon. Here's how it went in his words: "I had done the research and fixed a price in my head. I knew that the car was going to go fast, and I was going to look cool driving it. Then one day, I arrived early to a chamber of commerce mixer that was right next to the dealership, so I wandered in and let the salesperson run me through the car. At one point, I asked for the price and when he gave it to me, I said, 'I'll take it.' Clearly my subconscious took over and spewed those words out of my mouth. You see, the price was below my target. I bought that one-car-only-at-this-price car that was going into their ad. I never made it to the mixer that night, I was too busy buying the car."

Mitigate Decision Fatigue

Hundreds of decisions demand your attention every day—from the outfit you choose for your morning teleconference with clients, to the order in which you answer and sort your business emails—and every single decision drains your reserves of mental and emotional energy. Feeling depleted makes you more likely to overthink everything, so the fewer choices you make, the greater your resources will be for the important decisions.

Hank has a way of doing that and having fun when we go out to eat. If the menu has lots of things that he would find appealing, he hands the menu back to the server and says, "I will enjoy whatever you feel would be appropriate for me today." Three rules: If there is something he *does not* want, he tells the server, and he can *never, ever* send it back. It's just like when mom made dinner: you are going to eat and enjoy and appreciate whatever she put in front of you that night. You also must tip well.

You can lift your burden of making constant decisions by setting up simple routines. Just like on the TV show *The Big Bang Theory* where each day was reserved for a particular kind of food. And you can look for ways to eliminate some decisions completely, like delegation, opting out of meetings and and best setting up standard protocol practices. We teach our clients the power of saying, "*no!*" and it helps them when they realize that it's a powerful, two-letter word.

By the way, here's the menu for the guys on BBT:
- Monday—Thai Takeout
- Tuesday—Cheesecake Factory
- Wednesday—Halo and Junk Food
- Thursday—Pizza
- Friday—Vintage Video Games and Chinese Food
- Saturday—Cereal & Dr. Who
- Sunday—Farmers' Market

Why did we add that here? Simple. We were able to now rationalize all the time we invest watching the show in reruns. Not that we ever overthought it.

Master the Art of Constructing Creative Constraints

Parkinson's Law states that your work expands to fill however much time we allot to it. For instance, a one-month deadline for completing a presentation means that that project will take you an entire month. However, a one-week deadline would give you similar results in a fraction of the time. For this book, we decided to publish it in October, but made the decision in March. Since this is our eighth book, we have a checklist of how to publish our books and we know (especially from our last book, *Partners in Everything*, where we were starting from scratch with all the content) that it should take us no more than five months from beginning to publish. If you do the math, you know that we began this book in earnest in May, not March.

Overthinkers unconsciously adopt this law to overthink everything and allow themselves to spend a week or longer worrying about a task that would only take an hour to complete. This is unduly stressful in addition to being inefficient.

By using creative constraints, you can give yourself accountability and bypass the lengthy process of overthinking. For instance, you can make a deadline for finalizing a decision. Set a phone alarm, mark the date in your calendar, or even reach out to a stakeholder and tell them when you'll get back to them.

Remind yourself often that you have a competitive advantage due to your mental depth. By taming your tendency to overthink everything, you'll empower yourself to use sensitivity as your superpower.

Here's one more way our books give you an example of our overthinking. With our first book, *49 Stupid Things People Do With Business Cards, And How To Fix It*, Hank was procrastinating and worrying that he was not giving enough information and worrying "when is a book done?" The decision was taken out of his hand when an event promoter said, "If you have a finished copy of your book—it has been published—by March 15, you can promote it on my stage to 250 people." Writing ended. Editing began. Book was published the last week in February.

Write Down Your Thoughts Once, Then Distract Yourself for 24 Hours

Both of us have used this effectively for years. When our brains think we are in conflict or danger, a built-in alarm system goes off internally to protect us.

One thing many have found success with is writing down your feelings and waiting at least twenty-four hours (or just a few hours if it's an urgent matter) before replying or taking any sort of impulsive action. Then, you put that draft away while you distract yourself with another task.

For example, let's say Hank received an email about a promotional product that was delivered incorrectly. He is upset, his heart starts to race, his breathing gets shallow, and he becomes hyper-focused on what went wrong, why it went wrong, and where does the fault lie. If he responds to the email while his brain is in *OMG mode*, he might say things he will regret later, which may then fuel the vicious cycle of overthinking.

Writing negative thoughts down takes the power out of them; you may often not feel the need to act based on your apprehensive and distressed thoughts once you've done it.

Practice "Specific Gratitude"

In psychology, it is known that expressing gratitude can increase our happiness. It can help us contextualize our frustrations against what we love and help us connect to something larger than ourselves whether that's other people, animals, nature, or a higher power.

But we find that repeating the same gratitude practice over and over again can become rote and diminish the returns. For you, it might start to feel like a meaningless chore instead of a mindful practice. So, you might like to practice something called "specific gratitude."

For example, Hank got to do this during the writing of this book because a challenge he was having with his back was solved without surgery. Instead of writing in his journal every day that "I am grateful for my health," he was able to write, "I am grateful that I woke up today without any back pain and have the ability to help my clients with a clear mind."

The idea is for you to stay focused on the now, instead of overthinking general abstractions. Tomorrow, you might still be grateful for your health, but you might specifically be grateful that you have enough energy for a wonderful walk in the hills.

Here's a quote from our friend Kody Bateman that talks about something that goes hand-in-hand with gratitude, appreciation: "Appreciation wins out over self-promotion, every single time."

Your Action Item ❏

Make a list of some things you would like to have happen in your business; ten should do it. Then list the reasons you think they have not happened yet. Create the list now before you move to the next paragraph. Seriously, *stop overthinking it*. Create the list before you read on.

Now that you have the list, look at it. For each item on your list, if "not having the money" or "not having the time" is the reason it hasn't happened yet, dig deeper. Continue to work through the list to move ahead.

* * *

And of course, if you can't stop overthinking to move forward, let's talk about it. We will take those blinders right off and get you on your path to success. Head to HowToGetThereFaster.com for your free 30-minute *get-the-blinkers-removed call* and we can talk about it.

Chapter 11

Your Sales Cycle: 10 Cautionary Tales to Improve Your Sales Process without Overthinking It

Hank here. Since my business past life is far more in the sales lane, this chapter is going to be in the first person. I am a student of the sales cycle. I have listened to many seminars where purchasing agents were the speakers. They all say that when you are in the purchasing position, you may think that you are in the *power position* but that is not always the case. When you are buying a product, you are also being watched by the person you are gaining information from. They know you may or may not buy their product, but they also know that in the world of business all things come around. At some time, you may be the one on the selling end of the sales cycle and be the one offering your product to the person that is currently selling to you.

To demonstrate this concept, I would like to share ten stories about the sales cycle that talk about how different companies have responded to what should have been easy business conversations.

1. Three years after buying it, the new owners of a very large factory in the promotional products industry are now contractually forced to change its name. As part of letting the industry know they are changing their name, they sent out a survey. The survey asked for very specific information and honest feedback. I responded but did not get the response that I had requested to my feedback. I have sold that company's products for three decades and if our business relationship was going to continue, I wanted to make sure my input was heard because it would benefit both their company and mine. A month after completing the survey, without a response, I had the choice of selling their Murphy's Law calendar or one produced by another company; I chose the other. They continue to be discussed in an industry social media group with everyone wondering "What happened to X company?" In fact, since they took over, it has been

51

obvious to everyone in the business that their customer service has tanked. They have made the sales cycle far more difficult and are losing sales because of it.

2.   I had a non-real-estate-related question for a realtor with whom I had done lots of business. I sent three emails asking if she knew a salesperson who name dropped that he had worked with her. She did not respond to say whether or not she actually knew them. A simple response was required, at best. Two (no) or three (yes) letters; still no response. Do I continue to refer to that realtor, especially when that city's market is filled with competitors?

3.   We had a handyman in our networking group. We needed our front doors refinished and I tried seven times to hand him the business without asking for a quote. He did not respond. In fact, within the group, three others said that they had the same experience. One of them said that she had referred a friend to him, and he did not respond. She said, "It makes me look bad." After the eighth non-response, we found someone else, and he did a great job.

4.   A home health care company asked for promotional product samples and pricing. After they received them, I followed up six times, but they did not respond, with either a yes, no, or still thinking. I then had someone ask me for a recommendation to a company like this home health firm for their parent. I could have referred this company, but I did not want to take the chance that this family, who had asked for my recommendation, would not be contacted. Ghosting a salesperson is never a good idea as a way to end the sales cycle.

5.   An insurance agent that we use asked us for coaching information. We provided it, along with a rather detailed description of what we would do for his firm. We gave him preliminary information on how we would assist his business. However, he had not informed us that this was going out for bids. We heard that we did not get the job when we heard that it was a bid situation. That would not have changed our pricing, but I know one thing—the lack of information makes it *certain* that when it is time for his renewal, we will be shopping it.

6. This one is a conglomeration. Sharyn is very active on LinkedIn. She reaches out to, and responds to, potential lead sharing partners every day. That means she is on teleconference or phone calls almost as often. It is amazing that there is a pattern of people who will either no-show her or give her less than fifteen minutes notice that something has came up. Today, a person who is a life coach and teaches piano, said that she had two back-to-back pupils and was Sharyn available later in the day. That was ten minutes before their call. Didn't she know that she had those students a few hours prior to the call?

7. Several months ago, I reached out to the president-elect of one of the chambers on which I sit on the board. Since we left Los Angeles for Sedona, she was the first president that I did not know prior to our move. My email said that I would like to get to know her and see how I could help in the upcoming year. She responded that she would get me three dates and times and we could pick one. In waiting for that call, I looked at her website and had a couple of ideas plus a couple of URLs that would serve her search engine optimization much better than the one she was currently using. She never sent the dates. But today, she left me a voice mail asking for sponsorship money for an event that the chamber is having next month. What would have been a definite, "*yes*" if she had connected, is now an "I don't know."

8. I caught myself almost doing this, too. I met a regional manager from Staples on a chamber of commerce networking teleconference. He offered to set up business accounts for me and offered a free gift with a minimum purchase. Since I needed a couple of solid-state external drives, I thought it was a good idea. But—I found myself getting busy and it took me longer than it should have to deal with the account set up. Writing this blog made me recall that I had not yet responded. I contacted them and we ironed out a few details. It ended well, and I now have two drives that allow me to store my photos plus an account with the company. And Staples lived up to their promise, as well. The free gift arrived promptly, as did my drives. They were on top of the sales cycle by making it easy to do business with them. Would you like a bonus gift for reading this chapter? It's simple: Just go to YourBonusGift.com.

9. Sharyn responded to a connection request on LinkedIn with, "Thank you for the connection. I'm looking forward to reading more of your posts and connecting." Five minutes later, she got a message: "That's great. I looked at your website and did not see any video. It's the best way to connect with potential clients. I attached a proposal that will show you how we can make your website better." Interesting come back. Especially since we have video on *every* page of our website. The lesson: stock responses, like stock photos, will make you look less than professional. The sales cycle will not be the same for all clients. In fact, the sales cycle can be slightly different with *every* client. It would have helped them move us through the sales cycle if they had looked at the Yuloff Creative website and our online footprint first. This happens to me constantly on Facebook as well. Remember to set up the relationship before beginning to sell.

10. One of our clients was hired to do some work for a retail store. It was a new customer to her, and she was very excited. She did all the preliminary work, which was three to four hours of effort. When they presented it to the owner of the store, he appeared to act as if he had not said, "*Yes, go ahead.*" (I saw the email. He did.) Did he change his mind? That is allowed, but why didn't he reach out and tell our client? This is a great reason to not do business on a handshake, especially with a new business relationship. I have learned this lesson way too many times in the past, and now share this tip with you. The sales cycle is not completed until you do the work. But it is also not finished until you get paid.

Here are questions for each of us when we are in both the buying chair of the sales cycle as well as the selling chair:
- Are you forthright when asking for information from a salesperson?
- Are you offering a fair deal when you are on the selling side?
- If soliciting information from multiple sources, do you let everyone know that the purchase has been made, even if it is not from them?
- Is it possible that you *ghosted* the salesperson who was following up after they did not hear from you?
- Do you look at this transaction as a one-off that will never have a different side?
- Are we all treating salespeople like we want to be treated? This is very important if we are going to be in business for a while!

How we treat salespeople during the sales cycle can say a lot about how we will be treated when we are on the other side of the table. I would love to blame Covid-19 as a reason for business owners getting behind on their email and returning phone calls, though this was a challenge far before that pandemic hit.

During a coaching call with a friend, Forbes Riley, she reminded us of a quote that we believe is from Iyanla Vanzant: "The way we do one thing is the way we do everything." It goes along with that other saying "Do unto others . . ."

We talk about the best ways to follow up during the sales cycle in a seminar on follow up. It's called "10 Biggest Follow Up Myths That Are Stealing Your Sales" and is on the Yuloff Creative You Tube Channel and website blog.

While we're at it, here's another quote we learned from our good friend Brett Labit: "What is the highest and best use of your time? And whether it is follow-up skills or any others, we would like to offer you something that will make everything else you do during the sales cycle easier.

Your Action Item ❑

Answer the six questions above regarding how you are acting in the sales cycle before moving on. Do not become a cautionary tale because you were overthinking your sales process. I know, it's hard to prove a negative so you're going to have to keep that in mind.

* * *

If you have a challenge with any of them reach out to us at HowToGetThere-Faster.com.

Part 2

Nuts and Bolts of How to Stop Overthinking Your Sales and Marketing

Chapter 12

The 5 Questions Most Small Business Owners Ask about Branding

As a small business owner, you are no doubt bombarded by emails and ads promising you something like a "bigger, better brand in seconds." When you opt in, they then attempt to sell you a consultation where they will help you choose your colors and design a logo.

As a personal project, we began to talk to dozens of these professionals and we realized we were always left with a queasy feeling in our stomachs. That's because none of them went deep when asking us about our business. Once they found out that we were business coaches, they all went to "business coaches need to look like . . ." What was *amazing* to us is that none of them picked up on the *"we're a team"* aspect of our business. We know that is important because for years, we have been using the benefit that clients get two sets of eyes and two brains as something that sets us apart from solo coaches.

To make sure it wasn't just about the coaching industry, we each began to book other calls and used some of our clients as the answer to "so what do you do?" We became a financial planner, a non-profit, a retail store, and other service businesses. It turns out, it had nothing to do with our being a small business coach. They all went right for the graphic image.

Let's look at the five questions we get most often from our prospects and new clients as we create their brand.

What Is My Brand?
The clearest way we can define this is: Your brand is what your customers say about you when you are not in the room.

It is the image they carry of you in their mind. When you read the word McDonalds, what do you think of? When you read the word Mercedes Benz, what do you think of?

This can also be an industry-wide brand. For example, what do you think of when I mention hypnotherapy? Or used car lots? Or high-end restaurants?

What Are The First Steps To Define My Brand?

We're going to need to know your story. Another way to think of this are the answers to these questions: "Why does our company exist? Who do we help? How do we do it? What is the driving force behind our company?"

An easy way to answer this question is—what problems do we help our customers solve?" Here is the best tip I can give you here: *Your prospects will run away from pain faster than they will run toward pleasure.*

What this means for you is that you can say, "We help professionals retire faster and easier," or you can say, "We help professionals avoid working hard for thirty years and having nothing to show for it." See the difference?

Here's another example: As business coaches, we tell two stories. First is that we are the *easy button* when it comes to systems to make all your marketing easier. We can also tell you that by holding your hand through the difficult marketing decisions, they will become easier. I prefer the easy-button image, but prospects *respond* more to the hand holding, which is great because it's something that most coaches don't do.

For those of you who love the most esoteric way to ask this question—what is your hero's journey that got you where you are?

How Do I Choose My Company Colors and a Logo?

There's a lot of information out there that has to do with the psychology of color combinations and how it affects the human brain in purchasing decisions. Is it all true? Some of it, probably (he said half rolling his eyes). But let me ask you a question: If there was *one* combination that worked more than any other in a *significant amount* . . . . Wouldn't all major companies figure this out and switch?

Here's my biggest tip: You must live with your logo and your color scheme; therefore you better love them.

When I design a logo for a client, I first show them their corporate name in many typefaces in black and white. I want their feelings to start before we add any color or symbols.

Then I show them the favorite choices in a few colors, after asking them what color pallet they love.

Then we add the visuals.

This has been the process for way into three digits of logos over the decades and it is *rare* that we must do a major revision within a period of many years.

How Do I Share This with My Prospects?

Another way to look at this question is—what is your voice? You share your voice using a lot of marketing tactics. Here is a small, basic list:

- The blog on your website
- The videos you use to support that blog and as stand-alone promotional pieces
- The ads you run in various places
- Press releases you send out to announce things happening in your business
- Each time you speak in public— that could be at networking events (elevator pitches) or webinars

Your brand will become an integral part of your marketing.

How Will I Know That My Brand Is Working?

The short answer: Test what you are doing with different messaging to different parts of your list.

The longer, more detailed answer: You must remember that your brand is what your customer thinks of when she reads your company name. The first way to see if your brand is resonating with your prospects is to look at your new customers after you begin to share your brand-enhanced messaging in the world.

When we run our Small Business Breakthrough Bootcamps, we will look at the registered attendees, cyber stalk them and figure out what their collective challenges are going to be. We also *ask* them prior to the event what they are hoping to learn. Based on the answers, we can then change the content of the bootcamp to address their perceived needs. A way you can do this without following our bootcamp model is to survey your clients and, if possible, prospects who don't buy from you as well.

When you begin to see your client base change to be the type of clients you most want to serve, you will know your brand is resonating with your prospects. If not, then you must change your outgoing messaging or tell your story in a different way.

An Important Point for Small Business Owners

Quite often, a small business will have us handle all or parts of their marketing (this can also apply to businesses who run ads on a radio station or a print publication). In those cases, having a written *brand guide* can be a helpful thing to give to your vendor.

Your brand guide covers everything that has to do with how your company is presented. This can include:

- Your logo and the way it appears
- The color pallet that is acceptable
- The size and placement of your logo compared to all other content of the piece
- The way your company name and others mentioned in the recording is pronounced
- Your slogan
- Your mission and vision statements—we'll cover this in another chapter
- Key words that should be used when describing your products or services
- The contact person who can answer questions about anything that has to do with marketing your company

Your Action Item ❏

Do a deep dive to answer the question—what is my company's brand image? Include in that discussion—how do our clients see our company?

* * *

When it comes to branding your small business, we know that this is a fuzzy-how-to-do-it challenge. To assist you in getting focused faster, we would like to offer you a *free marketing consultation.*

We'll discuss where you are in your business right now, where you'd like to go, and how you might get there much more quickly without getting sucked into the vortex of conflicted advice floating around in the world and in your head. There's nothing to buy on this diagnostic call. No gimmicks and no nonsense. The website where you can schedule your call is www.HowToGet-ThereFaster.com.

Chapter 13

What Are the 12 Types of Videos You Can Create Now

You have an opportunity to reach out to your potential clients and customers with a marketing tactic that they want to utilize and that most of your competitors are not going to use. Two thirds of the population prefer to learn important information from a video format. What that means for you is that your clients would like to see you in action. The more you shoot, the more comfortable you will be in front of the camera. As the O'Jays said in 1975, let's "give the people what they want." (The Kinks said it six years later, too.)

Here are twelve types of videos that you can create right now to promote your business:

1. Video tips about topics that you are an expert in or that involve your business.
2. Product reviews if you have a book or product solely for the purpose to introduce and share features of a particular product.
3. Promotional video that talks about something you're selling or offering for free.
4. Interview with you being interviewed or you interviewing someone or just a joint video with another complimentary business professional on a topic you both have expertise in.
5. Testimonial video for someone else (or request them from your clients). Your website and every sales page *must* have video testimonials.
6. Training video for one of your paid courses or programs.
7. A free webinar or preview call designed to teach a little, list build, get people introduced to you and then make offers to work with you, enroll in a program or come to a free discovery/strategy session with you.
8. Facebook live or other social media live video with the purpose of

building relationships and having your followers get to know you.

9. Rant videos . . . if you must, go ahead and share some controversial thoughts!

10. Webpage videos—these are videos that would enhance the wording on a specific page on your site. These could be good for the following types of pages (literally every page could have an explainer video): home, about, services, free gift, contact, free consult, thank-you pages, speaker page and more!

11. Tutorial video—either doing this for free or paid (I've done both). Some I feel have more value that I charge for, others that could be a very good draw to get more people on my list, I may give away. (Some tutorials are good to show your assistants what you want done, or in reverse, they may create one for you to show things that would help you improve your business.)

12. The thank-you video—"Saying think you is more than good manners; it is good spirituality." Alfred Painter. Use this as your guiding light to send individual messages to those who have and continue to help you.

Your Action Item ❏

What is one video you can create for each of these twelve types of videos? What will you be discussing? If you don't, for example, have a paid course or program, double up on one of the other twelve so you have a big list to start with. Add a date you will shoot the first one and add a deadline for when you will finish the entire twelve.

* * *

Do you want help with this project? We are a link away. FreeMarketingConsultation.com puts you into our calendar to get started with this and other marketing projects that will build your business now.

Chapter 14

Tips for Making Your Video Backgrounds Better

Your video background can be as important to your video as the actual content itself. Why? Distractions! There are many things which go into creating a new video and making it as attractive as possible. In this blog and the video that goes with it, we will discuss what is going on behind you.

If you don't think your video backgrounds matter, look at your television screen. It's why cable news channels and interview shows spend hundreds of thousands of dollars and build impressive sets. So, let's all make sure *our* backgrounds are professional.

In our office we have two places where we shoot our videos. The first is in our radio show studio. It is also set up with lights and three back drops— black, white, and green screen. The second is our *war room* where we work with clients. If someone else owned our house, it would be their living room, but we put our conference table, some comfortable chairs and three very large white boards and see through blinds. These blinds allow us to use the light in the room and to have a light background of the red rocks behind us and both stay in balance.

Whether you are shooting in your kitchen, your office, or any of your public spaces, pay close attention to what is behind you. Plain walls are the best, though many people also use a filled bookcase with few knickknacks. We have heard from many people that they look at the books on the bookcase to try and get an idea what you are like, so for your video backgrounds in your library, beware, or plan for what they will be reading in your video backgrounds.

If you are using your laptop camera, make sure that the camera is at forehead level, so you do not get the point of view of an ant looking up at a giant. You should also know that turning your laptop and your camera just a little bit can make a huge difference. If your camera is pointed up, the lines of the wall and ceiling can be striking and distracting. Pay attention to those angles. If you turn your computer in the wrong direction, you can have the sharp angles of walls that make your video look busy.

Another important point for your video background is the placement of your head in the frame. Make sure that there is nothing growing out of your head, like part of a wall or a post. Tree limbs and branches, if you are outdoors or even if they are on the outside of the window, make you look funny. Shelves from your bookcase can seem to cut your head in half.

If your video background is a wall and you have lots of awards on the wall behind you, they'll give you third party validation, but they're very busy. Your viewers will not pay as close attention to you because, like the books in your library, they will wonder what the awards are for and from whom.

If there are two of you in the same video shot, sitting next to each other, take some practice shots to make sure you are both in the shot. Most of the time, we have to sit knee-to-knee, so the side of the video does not cut off our heads vertically. This is one time when your video background may not be as important because with two of you in the shot, there is not as much space in the frame.

Instead of using a video camera, I love using an online tool like Google Meet to create my videos. The benefit is that the upload time is almost nothing because Google has built the filters into its Google Keep product. If you are using an online tool where you can determine which camera is dominant, pay attention to which camera stays in the large screen at any one moment. Don't forget to click back and forth if you do not use the automatic feature. At the end of the video, you also must click to the view of yourself before you sign off. Remember, too, that if there are two of you in different places, your video backgrounds are doubly important because there are two of them that are bouncing back and forth in the viewer's eyes.

The lighting you use is very important. Fluorescents and natural sunlight cast different parts of the light spectrum, so be certain your camera is set for the proper light, or you can look very green under indoor lights and severe shadows can put a line right down the middle of your face if you are outdoors.

Your Action Item ❏

Take a good look at the place you are shooting your Zoom solo and group calls. How are you showing up? Use this chapter to come up with a list of three ways you can improve. Make those improvements immediately.

* * *

If you want help preparing videos for your marketing, you can always connect with us at www.HowToGetThereFaster.com for your free 30-minute break-through session where we can go over how you look.

Chapter 15

Your Overthinkers Guide to AI and Writing

In the summer that this book was written, there was technology that was all the rage in business circles. It's a product owned by a company called OpenAI that theoretically writes your content for you. I am about to take a stand on this product and others like it, and I will prove my point with a list you'll find several paragraphs below.

In addition to creating content, what it also seems to be doing is stealing content from other sources on the internet or making up facts that don't exist. The people who want to sell you courses on how to use it to your best advantage say that you simply must train it and for a price they will teach you how to ask it the right questions to avoid all that unpleasantness.

Most of the businesspeople that will admit to using it say, "I only use it to give me ideas." And, "It points me in the right direction." What they don't say is, "I'm too lazy to do my own research and writing."

I am a believer in the phrase "never say never" but we will never use those apps. We gather research from lots of sources. We add quotes. We do all the things that writers do. But we write it all ourselves and always suggest that our clients and you do the same. You see, when people read our books, they have questions about what they read. If we didn't write the book, we couldn't answer your questions, and as small business coaches that eliminates the three purposes of writing books:

1. To give you information that you will use to build your business. This leads you to refer us to your small business owning friends for coaching.
2. To entice you to work with us to successfully build your own small business.
3. We use content as special reports and exercises that we give away to small business owners like you who set appointments with us.

Your content will do the exact same thing for you.

For any of the above three reasons to happen effectively and successfully, you must be able to demonstrate your abilities as a thought leader in your industry, not someone who can program an app to do your homework.

As I write this, I think there is a fourth reason we write books: It's a place to compile all the content we are constantly creating. We do not have the challenge that we hear incredibly often of, "I don't have time" or, "I don't know what to write about." (Jump to the bottom of this chapter, we have a solution for that.) This book contains content that was written specifically for this book (like this chapter) and some that has appeared as special reports we use in our business as well as on our blogs and social media pages.

And now to my proof. Here is a list of short phrases you have probably used in your writing and when you speak to friends. Take a look and tell me of the phrases on this list how many have you used?

- Knock, knock! Who's there?
- Set your teeth on edge
- Heart of gold
- Faint hearted
- So-So
- Good riddance
- Fight fire with fire
- Seen better days
- Too much of a good thing
- Send him packing
- Wear your heart on your sleeve
- Come what may
- Not slept a wink
- The game is up
- For goodness sake
- What's done is done
- Come full circle
- Baited breath
- Green-eyed monster
- Laughing stock
- Vanish into thin air
- Be all /end all
- Dead as a doornail
- Out of the jaws of death

- In a pickle
- Fair play /foul play
- Brave new world
- Makes your hair stand on end
- Break the ice
- Breathed his last
- The world is my oyster
- Wild goose chase
- Love is blind
- Lie low
- Naked truth
- A sorry sight
- Heart of hearts
- A piece of work

I tested this with 378 people over twenty-four hours on our social media pages and the average number of "*yes*" answers per person was thirty-two which is over 80%.

Now—here are twenty-four slightly *longer* sayings. How many of *these* have you heard or used when writing or speaking to friends?

Be not afraid of greatness. Some are born great, some achieve greatness, and others have greatness thrust upon them.

- Uneasy lies the head that wears the crown.
- Nothing can come of nothing.
- What's done can't be undone. (Or What's done is done.)
- To thine own self be true.
- The devil can cite Scripture for his purpose. (Interestingly, I heard this on the news just last night.)
- What is past is prologue.
- Neither a borrower nor a lender be.
- All that glisters is not gold.
- The fault . . . is not in our stars, but in ourselves.
- I like this place and could willingly waste my time in it.
- Brevity is the soul of wit.
- Conscience does make cowards of us all.
- Jealousy is the green-eye'd monster
- If we are true to ourselves, we cannot be false to anyone.
- Be great in act, as you have been in thought.
- Suspicion always haunts the guilty mind.

- All things are ready, if our mind be so. (I think this is where Napoleon Hill got his famous phrase, "everything the mind of man can conceive it can achieve.")
- Many a true word has been spoken in jest.
- Thought is free. (Hmmm . . . inspiration for the U.S. First Amendment?)
- Don't waste your love on somebody, who doesn't value it.
- Misery makes for strange bedfellows.
- Lord, what fools these mortals be!

Those phrases and sayings are each at least 407 years old. They were penned by William Shakespeare and are still in common use today.

Our point is that the odds are very long that I write something that is going to be in common usage four centuries from today. However, if you are using your writing to generate business in your own lifetime, the odds go way down, and your chances go way up. But they need to be your words because your prospect's subconscious must recognize your syntax as yours when they meet you. Otherwise, the cognitive dissonance will tell them that something isn't quite right, and your sales opportunities plummet.

If you do decide to use these programs, remember that a content writing bot is like hiring an intern you have working for you. You *still* must check his work to make sure that it represents your voice.

Don't dilute your thoughts. Start and continue to write.

Your Action Item ❑

Begin to make a list of things you want to write about. You will use them in your blog, as special reports that prospects will want so much, they will set appointments with you to get it as a bonus, and as articles you will send to magazines that cover your industry. When published, they're a great way to get third party validation.

* * *

If you are stuck on what to write about, we have a simple exercise to bring you through. All you must do is set your free 30-minute appointment with us at HowToGetThereFaster.com and we will explain it to you and help you get started.

See what I did in that last paragraph? I showed you how to do what I alluded to in the third reason to write. Your turn!

Chapter 16

The Power of Your Frequently
Asked Questions

As I began the blog that this chapter is based on, I realized I was having the exact same reaction that many of you have—what do I write about? When Sharyn and I speak in front of small and large groups, of almost every type of business organization, the answer to that question is almost universal, "I would blog if I knew what to write about."

I think that most of you *tell* us that instead of the real reason which is, "I don't have (or I don't want to make) the time to write a blog." *A* blog. As in just one.

"Oh, goodness," many of you say, "you want me to *keep* blogging?"

It's alright, you are in good company. In fact, I had no idea what to write. I could not think of anything, so I went back to the starting point. And I am going to give you a shortcut for how to do that towards the end of this chapter.

That starting point is—what do your clients always ask you? In this case, it's what do I blog about? (Which is the first question we get to right after, "do I *have* to blog?")

The important thing to remember is that this is a Google world. Your prospects are looking for you. And they are using Google to do it. They are also using Google's subsidiary and the second most used search engine, YouTube. Therefore, it is important that you put together a list of the questions that your potential clients are asking Google, as they try to figure out if you exist and where you are. Those questions will be your first blog posts.

As for that shortcut I promised two paragraphs before, here it is. Those questions, with shorter answers, will be repurposed as your *frequently asked questions* section of your website. We suggest your list have ten questions that they ask you all the time, and another ten questions that you *wish* your potential clients would ask you.

If you ask Google about FAQ pages, you'll find quite a few examples of recommended page layouts. For most small businesses, the Microsoft layout is probably the best and the easiest to set up.

What is most interesting about this method is that it makes you focus on your business and your sales process. Imagine having an opportunity to take a deep dive into what you are doing to generate more sales and make corrections that will speed up your process.

If you Googled this topic and came upon the blog this topic was based on, you are having challenges beginning your blogging process. Here are a few questions that you can adapt to your business:

- How does someone know you are the right one to solve their challenges?
- What sets you apart from your competitors?
- Who are the businesses that most easily benefit from our service (or product)?
- What is the easiest way for us to work together? In person? Online? Phone?
- What are the first three steps you take a client through?
- What are the most beneficial features of your product for me?
- What are the various programs you offer?
- How much does it cost for each program?
- What payment methods do you accept?
- What is your guarantee or return policy?

Your frequently asked questions list can be better than your competitors in three ways. The first is to answer their questions directly and quickly.

The second is to add a short video to each of those questions. These videos should be as brief as possible. Two thirds of the population would prefer to gather their information by video so you are doing them a favor (and yourself since these videos will help increase your Google ranking, assuming you are using YouTube for these videos).

The third way to make the frequently asked questions section work for you is to mention that for each of the questions, there is a longer, more thorough explanation in your blog and you can create an internal link from your FAQ section to each of your FAQ blogs. Those internal links and each of those videos also help you a lot with your search engine optimization.

Your next step will be to periodically share links from each of those frequently asked questions to your social media platforms. The idea is to boomerang people from your business pages to your website.

Any time you create content for your website, you are helping your business. And when you can repurpose that content, it makes the time you invest in writing it worth even more.

Your Action Item ❏

Create your list of frequently asked questions. This usually takes about thirty to forty-five minutes.

* * *

When you want help in creating your own FAQ section, please go to www.FreeMarketingConsultation.com and book your free, no obligation, 30-minute *success call* with us.

Chapter 17

26 Ways to Repurpose Your Content and Increase Your Sales

Creating content is one of the three best ways to build your business. It's the only one of those three that takes the time you invest in it to give you a twenty-five-fold return on your investment. That is an amazing return on your investment. How does that happen? All you must do is repurpose your content into other forms, both in writing and as videos.

We tell our private coaching clients all the time that when they have gone through the trouble to create content, you should be proud of yourself. Most of your competitors are not creating content. We remind them that there is an old saying that "you will get paid for doing those things that others are not willing to do."

But being proud of yourself is not a means to an end. When you repurpose your content, it will increase your audience and readership by sharing your content to as many places on this list as possible. That second chance might lead to your first chance to gain a new client.

Here are two caveats: If you are already a content creator, as you go through this list you may want to repurpose your content by jumping right into using all of them. We suggest you take one or two and get focused on those before getting into all of them. If you are not yet a content creator, we hope that this will allow you to see all the reasons you should begin to create content as a way to promote your business.

Before we get into the *how* to repurpose your content, here are four reasons *why* repurposing helps:

First, repurposing your content improves your search engine optimization as people look for what you wrote about. When you have tagged your content properly, it can allow the search engines to match the searcher with you and your business.

The second reason to repurpose your content is that it helps you reach customers when and how they *want* to be reached. You have your content. You post it. You properly tag it. They type your tag into the search engine, and you are delivered to them.

Next, when you repurpose your content, it increases the impact and the retention of your message.

Lastly, when you repurpose your content, it allow you to quickly test in which ways your audience prefers to get your content.

Let's go through twenty-six ways that you can use to repurpose your content and generate more interest in what you do, and through that process, increase your sales.

1. *Content for your podcast.* On a weekly basis, we pulled material from our blogs as segments on *The Marketing Checklist* podcast. We also turned segments originally written for the podcast *into* blogs.

2. *Content that you offer to other podcasters by being their guest on the topic.* Having several topics that you can offer podcasters makes it easier to get booked.

3. *After you have been on that podcast, create a transcript of your segment.* This becomes a second blog on the original topic. As you read lower, you will see why this is content-creation gold.

4. *A guest blog on another company's website.* Our networking group has a blog and we tell our members that we will repurpose your content by publishing their blogs on the group's website.

5. *Your segment in someone else's webinar or summit.* We were recently invited to share a twenty-minute segment on the Authority Marketing Summit and spoke only about public relations. I went back to a blog I wrote years ago for our bullet points and updated them. If you plan your presentation correctly, you can add several boomerangs which brings the listeners to your website and landing pages.

6. *Social media posts—text (a sentence or two with a link back to your blog).* This is a boomerang post to get people to your site. We do this on our Facebook page (FB.com/YuloffCreative). Adding the entire blog is not the way to share your brilliance because we want to get people to your website instead of lingering on your social media pages, where there are competitors lurking.

7. *Social media posts—visual information.* Pinterest (hey, go like our page, OK?) is an entirely visual medium. Take your bullet points and

turn them into an infographic. Or create a separate meme for each point.

8. *Social media posts—visual quotes to photos.* Take a quote from your posts and add it to your photo making it into a visual post for all your social media profiles.

9. *Social Media posts—visual quotes to memes.* Put several quotes on one meme to share for all your social media profiles.

10. *Updating your past blogs, your past content.* By updating your blogs it allows you to think of new content to add to that blog. This gives you more SEO credit (see our blogs about SEO to see why). I recently began updating our past blogs and have added an average of 250 words to each blog. Longer blogs are better for your SEO than short blogs. This will also bring you to another SEO improvement . . .

11. *Add links, forward links, from past content to newer content on the same subject.* Google loves internal links. From Google's point of view, it rewards the people who use their search engine with even more information than they expected to get when they used the search. By the Google way of thinking, if the search result delivered more to the user, that person will come back and use Google again. And that gives Google advertisers more exposure. And *that* gives Google a chance to sell more advertising. It all comes back to advertising! Google very much wants you to repurpose your content.

12. *It becomes the content for a video on your YouTube channel.* There are ways to make this more effective, focusing on the proper tagging and description that you include with your video.

13. *A chapter in your book.* Roughly 70% of the chapters in our books began their lifetime as blogs. When you are blogging, you have multiple ways to repurpose your content, and writing books is one of the most profitable. When we add them as a chapter, it takes less time to rework the blog than write the chapter from scratch. It is how we were able to get *The Marketing Checklist for Sales: 49 Easy Ways to Improve Your Sales for Professionals Who Don't Like Selling* ready for editing and publication in less than a fortnight.

14. *E-book.* Have you written three or more blogs about one topic? You now have an e-book on the subject. Every book you write takes a big

step forward towards being seen as an expert on the subject.

15. *Create different levels of content.* Your potential clients are going to come to you with three expertise levels—beginner, intermediate, and expert. You can take *any* of your blogs and *triple* the amount of content you get on the subject by creating these levels. We have done this with our social media webinars. We have a beginner, an advanced, and a hands-off level where we give our watcher just enough information to hire someone to do it for them.

16. *Create different levels of content, upgrade.* Take the above tip and create a content upgrade. A content upgrade is an in-depth dive into the shared information that takes your reader to the next level—and that you share in exchange for an email address.

17. *Create different levels of content, upgrade your podcast.* Take the above tip and create a content upgrade for your podcast. In this case you are taking the listeners of your podcast to the next level—and that you share in exchange for an email address. You will need to get them to a landing page prepared for this broadcast.

18. *A free report used as an opt in for your website.* Even your most rabid fans are not all that interested in signing up for your newsletter. They *do*, however, want your free report.

19. *If you do create a newsletter, your blogs can be part of it.* Perhaps just the bullet points, like a "Top 10 ways to . . ." and then send them to your blog for more information.

20. *A free gift when you are a guest presenter anywhere.* Your job as a guest on someone else's stage, whether is in person or on a webinar, is to give their listeners enough information that they also become *your* listeners. Think about it. There are people in your industry that you follow, that you turn to, for information. How did you first learn about them? In some cases, they were guest presenters that you chose to follow. We have two favorite gifts that we offer, and we will share them with you here. The first is a free 30-minute success call where we solve your challenges. The other one is a year's worth of social media content that you can get at www.YourBonusGift.com. We invite you to collect one or both.

21. *A webinar on the topic or part of a webinar.* Over a dozen of our webinars began as blog posts. The blog was the roadmap and all we

had to do was create the slides. If you record the webinars like we do, then you have already created another way to repurpose your content.

22. *Write an email about your blog with a link that brings them back to your website.* This is a tactic we use *every* week. If you are fortunate enough to be on our mailing list, you will know that we have new content. Free content. Free content that will build your business if you pay attention.

23. *A video tutorial that is part of your online product.* We have created *a* lot of videos based on our blog posts. Some of them have become part of The Small Business Marketing Plan that we offer online.

24. *Sharing your stories.* When we were guest presenters for The Promotional Products Association International national convention, one of the questions from the audience struck a chord. I had *just* the story that would answer their question in a very concise way. It had to do with boxer shorts, a bank, and their advertisements. In this case, I used my more than thirty years of owning a promotional product company to make our point.

25. *Interviews.* When you interview thought leaders, clients, and business experts on your podcast, you can have the interviews transcribed and they become ready-made ways to repurpose your content. This is the easiest type of content to repurpose because it was the easiest to create. All you did was ask the right questions of your guest. Ok, so there is more to it than that, but it *is* one of the most fun ways to create the content. We have had guests on about a quarter of our 243 podcasts and when we changed the podcast to a view cast—*The Marketing Checklist Viewcast*—we changed the format to only include interviews of successful people. If you would like to be on our View Cast, just go to TheViewCast.com website, read the rules for being a guest and send us an email. This is the one way that we have yet to do ourselves. Content creation has never been difficult for us, so we have not had to rely on this method. We estimate that we have two or three different books worth of content in our interviews.

26. *Update your books.* If there are books that you have previously written, create an updated edition. I was talking to a client that had published a book seven years ago. I asked him if his point of view had

evolved since the publication of his book. He said there had been an evolution, but more importantly, he had more to say on the subject, but not necessarily enough new content for a new book. My next suggestion was that in the updated book, he could change the cover and add a photo of himself, since he was not on the original cover. You can add information to your book and issue an updated edition.

Here are a five ways you can promote that new edition:
  * A revised edition with (. . .) pages of new content
  * The 2023 Edition (or whichever year it is)
  * A new edition with a foreword by . . . (get a well-known person you have connected with to write one)
  * An updated edition including an online workbook (you would add the link inside the book)
  * Add a new (or updated) resources section

Here is a bonus for this last tip: While you are re-working your book, you can begin to promote it if you update the cover, first!

Your Action Item ❏

Whether you have been a blogging fiend, or despite all your best intentions, you've never written a blog, create some content. That's 500 to 1,000 words that talk about something you do within your business that shows you are an expert. Then choose *three* of the twenty-six ways listed in this chapter and get to work repurposing it. That's just over 10% of the ways we gave you, so it should not be that difficult for you. If you have not written the content, give yourself about an hour to ninety minutes to get that done, and another hour for the repurposing.

* * *

Want to discuss any part of the process? Reach out to us at HowToGetThere-Faster.com and we will get you on the best track.

Chapter 18

Here Are Ten Prospecting Mistakes You Are Probably Making Right Now

Since I made my very first sales call as a junior at San Diego State for The Daily Aztec until this very moment decades later, I have found one thing in common for almost every businessperson, whether they are in the sales department or not: The number one least favorite thing almost every one of them hate is to prospect for new business. The problem is that they make mistakes that make their job harder. And when you make prospecting mistakes, it makes your sales job a lot harder. And when your sales job is harder, you don't want to do any prospecting for new business.

Prospecting Mistakes

1—Don't Ignore your prospecting's inner thoughts, goals, and dreams.
The thing that most salespeople forget in the sales process is that it cannot be about them. You must focus on your prospects needs. The average person will run away from something painful faster than they will run toward something pleasurable.

2—Using the same message multiple times.
When I started as a sales manager and then as a small business coach, I was shocked to see how common this mistake was. Salespeople and small business owners send the same social media and email messages over and over, and mail repeat direct mail pieces to the same people. Often, you just need to change the message. What we teach our coaching clients is to remember that it's all about testing.

3—Prospecting inconsistently.
Prospecting should be done on a regular basis for several reasons. First, it allows you to build momentum. Second, it makes sure you avoid the feast-

or-famine cycle which wreaks havoc on many service professionals and retail companies. Third, it allows you to systematically test your approaches to see if one works better than the other.

4—Selling too early in the process.
This is good news because it means you don't have to be pushy to be a good prospector. My God, don't you hate it when you meet someone, and they go instantly into some kind of sales pitch? Ugh. Because this is such an important concept, allow me to pull back a curtain for you here. I am so very hyper aware of the selling-too-often mistake that we go overboard in the other direction. When you are on our list you hear the word free a lot. Free blog. Free podcast. Free webinar. Free. Free. Free. Be of service, and your client base will grow as large as ours. We normally add this offer at the end of our blogs: Get your free 30-minute focus-your-business-now call by heading to www. HowToGetThereFaster.com. We aren't selling you a thing.

5—Not doing enough research.
A little bit of research is essential because it allows you to personalize your outreach. However, that brings me to my next point . . .

6—Doing too much research.
A balance must exist. Sometimes small business owners like you will procrastinate by researching their prospects and getting as much information as they can before making a move. We have two clients who continually get in their own way by thinking that they have to have every answer to every question they ask . . . or don't ask.

7—Focusing on closing.
I tell entrepreneurs to focus on opening instead of closing. Why? Because you could be the best closer in the world, but if nobody is in front of you, it doesn't matter. If you ever read a sales book that told you to focus on the ABC's of sales—meaning Always Be Closing—go get your money back.

I've found that a mediocre closer with a full pipeline can beat the pants off a great closer with an anemic pipeline. I know that one of our clients is going to read this, so I am leaving this message for her: It has everything to do with your list. If your list is big enough, the outcome with any one person on that list holds less importance. Now that you have read it, call me, ok? You have my cell number. Ok, now back to the rest of you.

8—Underestimating how many leads it will take to get a prospect.
Not too long ago, I had a private coaching client email me with a question about a direct mail campaign and he was shocked to learn that a good response rate for a mailing is around .5%.

He was expecting a response rate north of 10%. For that to happen, he would either need a highly qualified mailing list or he would have to be the greatest copywriter to ever live. That's why numbers one, two, and three above are so important.

9—Failing to adjust based on feedback.
There's no such thing as failure, only feedback. Yet, it's a mistake to get feedback and do nothing about it. This goes hand in hand with numbers two and three (again).

10—Trying to figure everything out themselves.
We created the Small Business Marketing Plan along with the Group + Coaching Program to help small business owners like you shorten your prospecting learning curve.

We heard from many entrepreneurs who complained about all the problems with training material out there. For example, most prospecting material is tactical instead of strategic. There are hundreds of blogs. Countless podcasts. Endless videos, yet, they only give little slivers of information at a time.

There was nothing comprehensive for business owners like you who want a roadmap to follow to establish and refine their prospecting process. Heck, in this blog you've gotten enough of the how to be more successful to be successful. If you are willing to act now, if you want help, if you want to be held accountable and given guidance, then maybe you'll want to reach out to us. We created the plan for you.

Prospecting Advice Tips
If all of this has not been enough, *here are six prospecting tips you can use immediately.*

This part of the book was written on Christmas Eve and we had Santa Claus on the brain. I bet you didn't know that Santa Claus is a client of ours, right? We have a video to prove it—send us an email and we will send you the video. Here is some prospecting advice from St. Nick himself.

1—Consider your personal brand when prospecting.
Santa is a master of branding. From his red suit and white beard to his jolly

personality and the iconic "ho ho ho," Santa has created a strong and memorable brand that has stood the test of time.

As business owners, it's important to also think about the image and message you want to convey to prospective clients. It would be a prospecting mistake to not ask the question what makes you unique and sets you apart from the competition? How can you effectively communicate your brand to potential clients and establish trust and credibility?

2—Improve your client (and prospective client) service.

In our Private + Group Coaching Plan vault of videos, our coaching clients got an entire video about this topic because improving client service has a direct impact on prospecting effectiveness.

How? Because it gets you thinking about how you can streamline your processes and improve every part of your business. Santa's delivery is faster than Amazon's, and his customer service rating is also higher.

3—Build your network.

Santa is also a master of networking and building relationships. He has a vast network of elves, reindeer, and other helpers who assist him in his mission to deliver presents to children all around the world.

As an entrepreneur, it's important to also build your network of professionals and resources that can help you serve people effectively. This can involve forming partnerships with other business owners or professionals.

4—Tell better stories.

Santa is a master of the power of storytelling.

Plus, the story of Santa Claus himself has been passed down for generations, and it's a story that touches the hearts of people all around the world.

It's important to think about the stories you can share with your clients to engage them and help them understand the value of your services. This can involve sharing success stories of past clients, explaining your industry's complex concepts in a way that is easy to understand, or using anecdotes and examples to illustrate your points. It's a huge prospecting mistake not to use stories.

Here's an example. In the promotional product industry, the artwork needed for promotional products is not the same as on your website or your social media. We are asking for a solid, real surface to do the same work as your screen and it's hard to understand. I came up with a great story to explain it to clients, based on the Troll Under The Bridge in the middle of the Artwork Forest.

There's also the story about Santa's elves and how they make your search engine optimization better. (We made a deal for our client Santa with Google to use the elves excess work capacity. It made the Google search engine so very much better than Bing, Yahoo, and all of the others. Ask us about how it can work for you, too!)

5—The core of most prospecting success comes from believing that you have something valuable to offer the marketplace.
This is a mindset issue. It's one of the very best things we do for you. Reach out and let's talk.

6—Make more lists.
Santa has a naughty and nice list. Good children get toys, and bad children get coal.

If you're not proactively identifying the right and wrong people for your business, you are wasting a large chunk of your time.

Your Action Item ❏
One of the best pieces of advice we can give you is that you should make a list of prospects and systematically approach them. Yes, I know this advice sounds simple, but the simplest advice often gets the best results. The trick is knowing how to structure your list and how to approach the people in that list. And for goodness sake, use a customer relationship manager to make it all easier. Need help with that? Take us up on the offer we put at the end of each chapter.

* * *

When it comes to making a prospecting mistake and creating strategies for your sales, we know that this is a challenge for most small business owners. The biggest challenge is that they want to get there faster. To help you get there faster, we would like to offer you a free marketing consultation. If you would like to get there faster, let's begin our conversation by increasing your profits.

We'll discuss where you are in your business right now, where you'd like to go, and how you might get there much more quickly without getting sucked into the vortex of conflicted advice floating around in the world and in your head. There's nothing to buy on this diagnostic call. No gimmicks and no nonsense. The website to schedule your call is www.HowToGetThereFaster. com.

Chapter 19

Lack of Follow Up Is How
They Lost the Sale

As a follow-up to the last chapter, we thought we'd give you a couple of stories where lack of follow-up is the number one reason that small business owners lose a sale. It is a well-known fact that in sales, it is rare that the first call results in a sale. You must continue to follow up and be available to answer questions so that lack of follow up does not cost you a sale. From time to time, we like to add another blog on our website that falls under the heading of "How They Lost the Sale." In this chapter, we want to share two stories.

Cautionary Story—How to Lose a Sale in Thirty Seconds

We are huge believers in nonprofits and what they do for your community. We have served on over a dozen boards, and Sharyn has an MBA in non-profit management. Each year we give well into five digits to support them and strongly encourage each of our small business coaching clients to find a nonprofit and support it monetarily, with time, or both. We even allow each client to choose the nonprofit of their choice to have access to our vault of marketing magic. With that in mind, we would like to share a story with you that happened when we attempted to put our nonprofit support program in place in a new state.

As new residents of Maryland, we wanted to get involved with local organizations, including making donations to some local nonprofits. We did a search through the database of LeTip (a national networking organization) because we were a top referring member of a chapter based in Los Angeles, California. We would get credit with the organization *and* get to do some good in our new local community in Maryland. (Mentioning LeTip as an organization should not in any way imply an endorsement of that company.)

Here's what happened. After a search, we sent an email asking for information about a nonprofit that runs a local arts festival in Columbia, Maryland. It was two weeks prior to Thanksgiving. For those of you who are reading this article outside of the United States, Thanksgiving is a Christmas-level holiday and doing business on that day is not expected. No sales calls are scheduled on this very family-oriented holiday.

A week later, after not receiving any response, we sent a second email. A few days after that, having had no response, we sent a third message.

The day before Thanksgiving, we finally got a message back through our scheduling link. The representative in charge of setting programs for the nonprofit asked if he could mail me information. I answered, "yes, go ahead and mail the information, and then we can talk."

The next thing I know, there is an appointment on our books—for Thanksgiving morning.

Interesting. We could not possibly have the information he wanted us to have that described what they do, so that we could make an informed donation decision by that time. Yet, there was an appointment.

Our thought was, "Well, what the heck." On that holiday, we got ready to accept a call that did not come. As is our practice, when someone who books time with us and it does not ring through, we call them in case they thought we were supposed to be the calling party even though our confirming and reminder emails clearly say to "*call us* at your scheduled time."

We called, and a person picked up the phone. "Hello, this is Sharyn and Hank Yuloff, you booked a call with us."

The reply was, "You got the wrong day. I thought I booked for next week." *Click.* Yes, he did not wait for us to respond. He hung up on us. *Seriously?* And, it gets better, read on.

When we got a follow up email an hour later, he was asking us to rebook the call at two specific times the following week. Times convenient to him, not when it would be convenient to us, *the donors.* We had to decide whether we wanted to rebook a call so that we could donate to his festival. What do you think we did?

This became the story of how a nonprofit reacted to a company reaching out offering to buy the service they offer. Their product was to show that we were connected to the community by getting promoted by a nonprofit organization.

You may not be a nonprofit. You may be a *for*-profit company selling your product or service. When someone calls you, how will you act?

How much other business is a poorly trained employee costing this nonprofit? Are you going to respond in a way that shows you appreciate getting a call? That you appreciate the chance to make a sale?

One of the lessons here is to understand that prospects connect with you in the way this is most convenient for them, and you must be flexible. The first time I got a message through Facebook asking for promotional products, I did not understand that. I was very annoyed that the client did not just send me an email. Boy, did I get that wrong.

If your prospect reaches out through phone or text or email or messaging on social media, get *back* to them by the same method. Make it easier for them and they will be more likely to do business with you because you made it comfortable for them.

If your prospect reaches out on a Monday, get back to them by Tuesday. Even if you are letting them know that you are incredibly busy with another client. You are letting them know that you recognize them and are going to get back to them at a specific time.

Then, don't miss your appointment time. Be prepared several minutes before jumping onto that video call, or phone call. Or be in the parking lot ready to walk in exactly on time. Better to be a minute early than even a minute late.

Just remember to *never* be the person who, because of lack of follow up, *got,* and *lost* the sale in just thirty seconds.

Now, as Paul Harvey used to say, here is the *rest* of the story.

When we have an appointment scheduled, our customer relationship manager (CRM) sends a series of emails reminding our prospect that they have a call coming up.

When the guy at the nonprofit got our emails, he did not just delete them. He went further. *He marked them as spam.* So not only did *he* mess up, but he also put a black mark in the system against our email address. He acted as if we had just reached out to blindly solicit *him.* Phillip Wiggensworth we were trying to give your organization money!

Cautionary Tale—Lack of Urgency Loses Commitment

Here's another case of poor follow up that cost a nonprofit a sale. In the past year, I had invested several hundred dollars in Linda's (fictional name) organization through attendance and sponsorship of their events. Here is the email conversation chain that began with me asking Linda about a new sponsorship program that her organization had begun to offer.

    Hank   "What if I want three or five minutes a month (the lunch or breakfast)?" *(This would have been an approximate $500 sale to the organization.)*

    Linda   "I am going to call you tomorrow and explain some changes and how I would like to market your events."

January 11

    Hank   "Only clear time to chat would be after 4 p.m. your time. My cell is 800-555-5555."

    Linda   "Hi Hank, I had personal meetings until just now, so I will reach out to you tomorrow.

    Hank   "Have a great night, Linda."

January 12

    Hank   "Starting to guess our conversation is not important."

January 13

    Linda   "I do want to talk with you and am noticing that it's hard to connect. I only work in the morning and have many personal/ kid meetings in the afternoons. Are you around this morning? Tomorrow before noon?"

January 14

    Hank   "I am clear 9-10 a.m. or 1-2 p.m. your time today. My phone will be with me."

January 18

    Hank   "Hi Linda, it has been a week since I requested a call after your email telling me that you wanted to discuss how we and the chamber were going to work together moving forward. I even gave you specific windows of time to call. If you are wondering why sales are not what they should be, it is a challenge in follow up.

January 19

    Linda   "Hi Hank, Thanks for getting back in touch. As you know, I only work part time in the mornings. The current office hours are 9 a.m. to 3 p.m. and I work within that time frame most days. I've been pretty busy planning and organizing the board retreat. It isn't anything urgent. I was just trying to touch base with you to understand your company and get to know you and see how we can be mutually beneficial to each other.

I'm in the office today from 11 a.m. to 2 p.m. If you have opening in your schedule, give me a call so we can chat. After today, I will be in the office Thursday and Friday from 10:30 a.m. to 2:00 p.m."

The question is: Where did Linda lose the sale? Was it lack of follow up? I posed this question to one of our private coaching clients and received this answer:

I'm going to say that it was in her lobbing the ball back to your court. Yes, her lack of follow up. She should have called you instead of telling you what her availability is and relying on you to chase her down. You made it clear you are ready to be sold.

Our client has absorbed our lessons like a sponge, and she was exactly correct. After that last exchange in the email chain, the budget for that project had been moved to another organization. Again, "Appreciation wins out over self-promotion every time." One of the simplest ways to show appreciation to a client is to take responsibility for being the one dialing the phone. Never take for granted that you have the client locked up.

There is a second important factor in this decision. And Linda did not know about this because I was never asked. It is, "How have we been performing for you? Have you gotten what you consider to be a better than adequate return on your investment?"

In this case, the answer was no. Linda's organization had not generated any revenue from me in over a year. Marketing theory tells us not to try something once and decide that it did or did not work. A twelve-month period is a very reasonable test period.

Some Final Words about Lack of Follow Up

Your sale is never done just because your prospect says, "I will buy." You must avoid lack of follow-up for whatever reason. Then you must fulfil the sale, follow up after the sale, and continue that process. This, I am certain, is one of the reasons that many salespeople are not as successful as they could be.

Your Action Item ❏

Go back to the last chapter. Implement those action items before moving forward in the book.

Chapter 20

(An Exciting Way) or (How) to Improve Your Follow Up and Productivity

Every week we improve the follow-up and productivity of clients and small business owners who take advantage of our free 30-minute get-focused success calls. Though they are from a very broad spectrum of business types and industries, we notice something similar with each of them. They all ask for three things, which I will share in a moment.

With the entrepreneurs who are speaking to us for the very first time, the first thing we do is find out more about their business by asking several questions. Their answers help us determine who their ideal client is, who they *want* to serve, and the marketing path that is the most appropriate for them. This gives us valuable insight into how we should advise them on marketing and sales tactics.

When we firm that up, we ask them how we can best help them that day. This is where they ask us those three questions.

First, if they are on the right path, they ask us, "What do I do next?" Or, if they are new to doing what they do, or the tactics we suggest are new to them, they ask "What do I do first?"

Most of the time, our answer begins with, "It depends," because there is no one path that every business can take that will get them to their nirvana, even if they are in the same industry and in the same part of the country.

After we give them their options to improve follow up and productivity, the second question they ask is "How do I get there faster?" Getting where you want to go with your business more quickly is a function of two things: First is how much time are you willing to invest in the project and second is how much of your time are you willing to invest in reaching your goals? Their path becomes clearer after we go through this exercise.

I should point out that during the time we invest with our coaching clients, their path may change. Things happen. Outside forces present options that can be very appealing. We are open to this because it happens in *our* business all the time. For example, we were honored to be asked by the social media site Alignable to be one of their very first ambassadors. Our role, along with a couple of dozen other small business owners around the United States, will be to help small business owners build their businesses using the Alignable platform. We will do it online and through in-person networking meetings. For us it is a way we can show leadership through example and to create opportunities in several communities in Northern Arizona. But this was a shift from our planned path and we had to make a change in where we were investing our time.

The third question, for those who are absolutely prepared to get started and are ready to get there faster is, "Will you hold me accountable?" We know what you are really asking is severalfold. Yes, we will hold you accountable to get done what you want to get accomplished. And yes, we will hold your hand while you get it done. And yes, we will be actively involved in your success. This is the most important part of the small business coaching we do for you and your business. We must show you how to get to the place you want to be. We help you create the *to-do now* and *to-do first* lists. We also create the *do-not-do* lists, which we have found sets us apart from a lot of coaches. These lists absolutely improve your follow up and productivity.

And there is one thing that we have begun to have our clients do.

So when you call us, in addition to your to-do list, where you get the positive feeling of, "*I did it!*" each time you cross something off, you should move those things that you crossed off, to an *I-did-it list*. This way, not only do you see things get crossed off behind you, but you will now give yourself credit for accomplishing things.

In addition to being a tool to improve your follow up and productivity, here is another important reason for your I-did-it list: Some of those things that you planned for, did, and succeeded in crossing off your list were *hard*! They took time. They took work!

We have begun to create these I-did-it lists for our own business and are immediately seeing the benefit.

This week we helped a client redo part of her website. And for another client we set up a social media page on Alignable. And for yet another client, designed a new logo. A fifth client used one of her 911-marketing-emergency calls (that come with our coaching program) to have us look at her presentation slides before a $50,000 presentation. It has been an exciting few days.

Yes, we crossed all those things off the lists we have for each client, but when we add them to the I-did-it list, we see how fast it adds up. The mental pat on the back you give yourself inspires you to get even *more* done. You are allowing marketing momentum work in your favor to improve your follow-up and productivity.

Another reason to create your I-did-it list is that it makes you feel really good! So why don't you try? Add an I-did-it-list sheet of paper on your desk. Start taking and giving yourself credit for the things you accomplish.

Now, if you want some help with learning to improve your follow up and productivity or anything else that has to do with your sales, your marketing, your human resources, and your back-office systems, we will show you how to get there faster and we will hold your hand if you want to know how to get there faster.

Your Action Item ❑

What is on *your* agenda for following up with clients? Do you have a systematized checklist that you go through? What is your time frame for following up with leads? Do you block out time? Using these questions, go through your prospect list and create a plan to follow up. As you begin to put it into action, create a plan for another prospect. You are starting a habit.

* * *

If you want to talk about them, go now to HowToGetThereFaster.com, and reserve your private spot in our calendar.

Chapter 21

How to Create Your Client Retention Plan

We have probably all heard the statistic that says that it costs between five and ten times more to get a new client than it does to retain one. And that is true. Here is an example. When we have a client *re-order* 250 t-shirts with their logo on the front and the back, the acquisition cost is zero, because the client has reached out to us. When one of our private business coaching clients renews their yearly contract, the acquisition cost is zero, so we are able to lower the cost of their business coaching investment, which we've done for more than a decade.

Like you, before we have a client, they must find us and get to know us. You had to take time to develop your clients too, right? In the drawing of an average sales funnel, you go through steps to have them get to know you. There are costs involved. It could be your time and an entry fee to go to a chamber event. It could be an e-mail marketing campaign which also takes your time and money to place the ads. It could be a direct-mail-marketing campaign which takes your time to design the piece (or hire a graphic artist) plus printing, preparing, and postage.

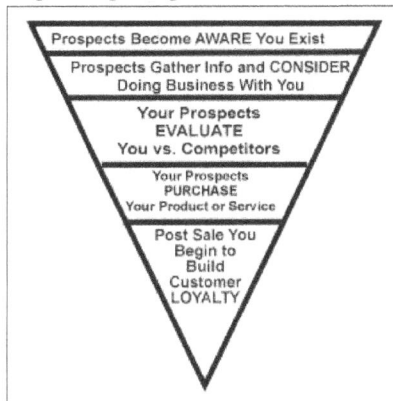

Prospects Become AWARE You Exist

Prospects Gather Info and CONSIDER Doing Business With You

Your Prospects EVALUATE You vs. Competitors

Your Prospects PURCHASE Your Product or Service

Post Sale You Begin to Build Customer LOYALTY

Once you have a client, it is in your best interest to *keep* them.

Let's talk about your client retention plan. What are you doing to make sure they are motivated to keep buying from you and your company? Another way to ask this is, "Do your clients still know, love, and trust you?" All our clients, and yours too, have lots of options in the world. How are you making yourself incredibly important and vital to your customer's success?

In our Small Business Breakthrough Bootcamps, we discuss the concept of *becoming a category of one*, which I believe was created by legendary E-marketer Dan Kennedy. When broken down, category of one means that you can niche down your potential clients so much that you are always the obvious choice. Even when they meet someone who is like you, offering services that might, on the surface, seem similar, they would stick with you because of what you do for them.

An important point to add here is that "I give them great service" is definitely *not* what we are talking about here. When we speak to audiences of business owners, we have had every one of them close their eyes while we ask them to do one thing: If you give great service raise your hand and keep it up. We always get 100% of the hands. Great service, and while we are at it, great pricing is something that every business says they do, so it is not a difference creator.

Let's look at six examples of client retention plans.

The first way to create your client retention plan is a rather easy one. Connecting on social media messaging. This is partnered with your text messaging, phone chats, and email. It is basically connecting with your clients in the way they want to connect. Add to this your promotion of your clients on social media profiles and you will move this ahead greatly.

The second tactic in your client retention plan goes along with the first. It is referring your clients to other clients or anyone you meet that you think would be a solid connection for your client. We try all the time to send our clients business. It will be a very definite way for your clients to see the tangible value of working with you.

This is a very easy thing to do when you keep it foremost in your mind to be a referral machine! Every month, we hold monthly marketing Mondays for a couple of different chambers of commerce. In those ninety-minute workshops we make a lot of new contacts with business owners. In that situation, we want to make a positive impression, so using this second tactic is important. We listen to those business owner's needs, wants, and desires and our antenna goes up if we can refer them to someone in our network that will help them. Recently, we met an allergy expert in the morning, and by the end of that afternoon, we had two referrals for her—an acupuncturist (they were later able to pass leads back and forth), and another business owner that happened to mention, "Sorry I am late, I've been sneezing all day—must be my allergies." When you are open to the business universe, you are rewarded. The bottom line is that one of them is now a private business coaching client.

The third tactic is to use business education—helping your clients develop their business by giving away some of your brilliance. We always invite our clients to come to our live two-hour workshops that we do for various chambers and to our Small Business Breakthrough Bootcamps. When they are there, we can talk about them and refer other attendees to them (this is an easy place for us to promote you). We also give business education through our blog which goes to our email list. You may be reading this because you are on that list. If you have ideas for other business education, send us an email at Info@YuloffCreative.com and let us know what we should write about. We use our podcasts and *The Marketing Checklist View Cast* as business educational opportunities as well. We always ask our audiences who has learned something new or remembered something that they used to know; the response here is also always 100%.

The fourth method you can use in your client retention plan is harder than you would think. It's called *just showing up*. It could be in the form of an "I was thinking of you. Thank you" text. You could send them a personalized card or appropriate gift. Making it personal is important.

We have a private coaching client that was expanding her quite successful sports merchandise company to add promotional products. How did we coach her to start from scratch? Show up in front of the local business owners. "Wow," you may be thinking, "she paid for you to tell her that?" Yes. Along with ideas on improving the sales in her first business, we had to remind her how she got her *first* business off the ground. Show up, show your products, make sales. It is the same formula, but a different industry. With our holding her accountable, she is off to a great start. And I got a new Red Sox jacket that is *way* cool.

Here is another idea that we witnessed during a recent Thanksgiving, and it is so good that we are thinking of utilizing it for ourselves and our clients. There is a realtor in our area named Karen Piet. She sends this email card to her clients offering a free pie for Thanksgiving. The kicker is that they must come to her office to get it. This gives her a chance to get her clients into her world and make them think about real estate. She gets a few quality minutes alone with them.

This leads us to the next marketing tactic for your client retention plan which is like number four and that is *actual human interaction.* If you are giving them that gift mentioned above, you might want to consider delivering it in person. You might want to pick up the phone and thank them for buying from you. Can you imagine getting a call from a restaurant that you went to for the very first time and it is the owner thanking you for coming and asking how everything was? How about getting that call from your dry cleaner? Or your dentist, chiropractor, acupuncturist, or podiatrist asking how you are two days later? *Yes,* this is time consuming, but it helps guarantee a return visit to your company, for a repeat purchase. You can also share tips on how to get the most out of your product or your service.

My optometrist does not make a personal call, but I *do* get a survey email each time I am there, asking how I enjoyed their service. They also, by the way, send a series of text messages confirming my appointments.

Last is to remember that at the beginning of this chapter, we talked about being able to niche down your clientele. That does not mean you have only one demographically or psychographically similar customer. You could have several avatars, or Harriets as we call one of our specific client types (Harriet is a female avatar of one of our target markets). You may want to split each of your segments into different Harriets so that you can connect with them on a more personal basis. Creating messages that are very personal to each of your Harriets will let them know you care about them and their business.

There is an old jazz version of the Simon and Garfunkel song called "Keep the Customer Satisfied." The first time I heard it was in high school, but it has always reminded me that our clients, *your* clients, are the entire reason for our businesses to exist. Let's let them know how much you care.

Your Action Item ❏

First make a list of your ten favorite clients. (You can define favorite any way you please—dollars invested with your company to their phone number makes you smile when you see it's them calling.) *Then* go back through that list and tell us what you are going to do to reach out and retain them!

* * *

If you would like some personalized ways that you can create your client retention plan, head to www.HowToGetThereFaster.com. After you take a short, easy survey, you will get an invitation to choose a time for your free 30-minute success phone call with us. We will know more about you and can help you create your plan. *That* is just one way we want to show appreciation to you for buying and reading this and all our other books.

Chapter 22

Seven Simple Ways to Get to Know Your Customers Better

"Get closer than ever to your customers. So close that you tell them what they need well before they realize it themselves."
Steve Jobs

If you want to better serve your clients, it helps to understand their expectations and behaviors. There was a major change, beginning with the pandemic, and with all the disruption and uncertainty of that year, your clients now have different needs than they did prior to 2020. It's important to get to know how business in many industries has changed so you can meet them where they are now. There are many affordable ways to conduct market research and get to know your customers better. Here are seven simple strategies to get valuable information about your clients.

1. *Analytics and data mining tools.* Make sure you use platforms that allow you to discern how clients are interacting with your website and emails. What pages do they visit most often? What emails do they open? We recommend looking for key information such as internet sources, the time spent on your site and how often customers buy from your site, if you provide that option. You may want to ask your clients directly what social media platforms and websites they like the most. When we do this with coaching clients, we look for patterns of behavior.

2. *Polls and questionnaires.* It is easier than ever to ask your clients a few quick questions about your products and services. Many customers are inundated with feedback requests. To get them to pay attention to your poll, consider incentivizing them with a small discount. And be sure to let your clients know how much you appreciate their input.

3. *Virtual focus groups and panels.* Online public opinion and research providers can help you put together sample audiences to source feedback. Do you want to reach buyers in the legal market, or the building trades for example? Get to know those target customer audiences to help guide your marketing strategies.

4. *Early access to new products.* Are you unveiling new products or programs? Allow your current clients first access and get their opinions on how you can improve these new offerings. This is an effective way to build goodwill and reinforce that their opinion matters. We use our books, like this one, to do just that. Our clients will get first access for free. Our prospects will get access to a couple of chapters free with a great offer. You may have just taken advantage of that offer. *Thanks!* Here's an offer *inside* an offer: If you did take advantage of that offer, email us within the first year of copyright publication and we will send you a preview of our *next* book, free! The working title is *The Physics of Marketing.* Your email address to use is Info@YuloffCreative.com.

5. *Targeted online surveys or quizzes.* Rather than sending out a blanket questionnaire to your entire client base, narrow down with specific audiences. This allows you to get a feel for specific needs and requirements for various groups, whether you are polling restaurant owners or medical professionals. For our clients, we even perform what is known as an A/B test where we change just a bit of information to see what pulls best.

6. *Customer recognition.* Another way to get to know your customers better is to feature them in your promotional campaigns. Invite them to provide feedback on industry trends or new concepts, and then give them a shout-out on your website or social media channels. Small businesses are especially keen on building online forums and communities around their brand specifically for the sounding board aspect. The easiest way to do this? Give them a shout out on your social media platforms. Say what you love about what they do or share a testimonial they received.

7. *Connect with industry thought leaders.* Want to know what leaders in a specific field are thinking? Ask to interview them for your

company blog or video series. Many experts are willing to share their thoughts and opinions in exchange for publicity.

Your Action Item ❑

Choose two of these methods and test them with someone in our client base.

The better you know your customers, the more you can anticipate their needs and the more value you can provide. Fortunately, you do not need a suite of expensive tools to conduct market research. Often, all you need to do is look for ways to communicate with your clients, whether you send them a quick poll or invite them to weigh in as part of a client panel. By taking time to build personal relationships, you will ultimately see better outcomes.

* * *

In other books and webinars, we describe in detail how to use your client's demographics and psychographic information to build these relationships. The information is all over our blog at YuloffCreative.com/blog.

If you need help doing this for you and your business, reach out to us at www.BoxFullOfMarketing.com and we can give you a free get-your-business-focused call.

Chapter 23

14 Ways to Show Your Clients Some Love

Every Valentine's Day we think that love may be fleeting, but there are still 364 other days left in your year to shower your clients, and your own business, with some heartfelt acknowledgement and appreciation.

This short 'n' sweet chapter will get you going in the right direction, internally and externally. Once you start down the list, you'll likely notice a few tactics you can expand upon.

For Your Clients
- Host a lunch-and-learn event. Invite attendees to bring a guest for free and send them off with a coupon for a discounted service.
- Recommend a book or white paper. Share your recently read white papers or business titles that you found helpful or insightful. We'll even send them a copy of any of our books for you! Just ask in an email!
- Pay it forward. Donate in your client's name to a cause you feel passionate about (or one you're pretty certain that they feel passionate about). This is a great way to connect clients to nonprofits and demonstrates your charitable side and community connectivity. We have a brand-new program we will be starting soon to help nonprofits generate more revenue. It's called the Non-Profit Partner Program.
- Share the social media love. Post a simple Facebook or Google Plus message, tagging your client and spotlighting an accomplishment or service that you value. It's free, takes less than a minute, and is sure to brighten your client's day with a burst of surprise positivity.
- Pick up the phone. A spontaneous check-in call to past and current clients to see how they or their business is doing, how their new grand baby is, how their child's college process is going—things you

paid attention to while courting but may have since forgotten about. Remembering and checking in shows that you are thinking about them outside of the current project scope or sales cycle.

- Send some sweets. Who doesn't love a good cookie, cupcake, or box of chocolate? Just buy enough for the recipient to share with coworkers.
- Be vulnerable. Invite honest feedback from your clients or customers. Let them know that you are continually aiming to improve their experience, and that for all the things you do right, there are certain areas where you're hoping to improve. Then sit back and let them lead the conversation.

For Your Business

- Rewrite your "About" page. Take the spotlight off you and focus on what you want your customers to gain by doing business with you. The new golden rule is to treat others as *they* want to be treated. Craft your "About" page to energize your current clients and to entice prospective clients.
- Add new testimonials. Reaching out to past and current customers or clients in a friendly, earnest manner—again putting the focus on them—is a good way to get feedback on what you're doing right, and wrong, and may lead to conversations about current needs and how you can help. When was the last time you asked someone for a testimonial? We have a script for it on our follow-up webinar.
- Get your taxes done. Early.
- Freshen up your services copy. Businesses evolve; does your website reflect the new skills and services you've added? Are there case studies or samples of work that you can upload directly to your site or to your LinkedIn and Alignable pages?
- We will take a look at them for you if you like. Just send us an email!
- Love thy network. Sending a friendly note of appreciation or thanks, or simply acknowledging that you've been reading their social media posts, love the content they're sharing, kudos for an award announcement, and chances are they'll remember this and repay in kind at a future date. We use a great service that prints real cards after you create it online.
- Update the look of your eNews. Revisit your digital newsletters from the past year, and along with your team, critique the use of white space, the font, the length of posts, the headlines and post titles,

and the quality of images. Then, compare your findings to those eNewsletters you have received and been impressed with. Where can you improve?

- Send a gift card. Gift cards are an easy, not-too-extravagant way to say "thank you" to industry partners who have referred you to new clients or have done a favor for one of your existing clients. Come to think of it, why not send out a few to your favorite vendors as well. These days, a few extra bucks, even if in plastic form, always comes in handy. If you are going to create a bunch of them, we can help you with that and include your logo on them as well.
- BONUS: Return an ancient email. This may seem silly, but the other day, I wrote back to a young man who's email I missed *six months ago*, looking for employment. He was so surprised and pleased; he replied with a very nice note and thanked me for taking the time to acknowledge his email. I still have a few others that I found in spam to take care of. I know I am not the only one.

I'd love to hear the different ways that you show your clients, and your business, some love, so send us your comments. And remember, your clients, and your business, are worth appreciating each and every day, not just on Valentine's Day.

Your Action Item ❏
Pick five clients and show them love using these methods. Try and use more than one so you get some experience with them.

* * *

Remember, you began your successful business with a plan. As you've grown, your path now has many possible directions. How do you focus and decide on the best one to take? How do you focus on what content to create, how to repurpose your content and where to share it? That's what we would like to do for you—show you and your business some love. If you're reading this, reach out at HowToGetThereFaster.com and we can have a love-filled chat.

Chapter 24

How to Pivot Your Business to Generate Sales During a Shock to Society

At the beginning of COVID-19, we wrote a report as directions for our clients; it was a very effective offer as a special report for opt ins on our website and during webinars. The pandemic was a shock to our society; it was not the first and will not be the last. It is relevant to learn some of the recent lessons from this event and contemplate how we would handle future societal shocks.

The pandemic was an *ultimate overwhelming situation* for those of us who have ever been overthinkers. In fact, we don't know *one* small business owner who *didn't* have an "OMG, *what do I do*?" series of moments. We spent most of the first several months recreating and redirecting the marketing paths for our clients.

What could be as bad as the pandemic? Here's one example: There is a prediction that when the next huge earthquake hits in the state of California, it could start in the south in the Salton Sea area and travel right up the San Andreas fault towards Northern California. During that event, for example, downtown Los Angeles would be under over twenty feet of glass as all the windows would pop out of the skyscrapers. Water would be cut off because the main water aqueducts cross right across the fault. It would cause hundreds of billions of dollars of damage and as the largest economy in the United States it *will* affect you, too. The state of Arizona has expectations and plans for 200,000 Californians entering their state. (For more info, head to Earthquake.usgs.gov).

We could mention some other situations that might be higher on the scale, but we're not going to put those in your mind.

To learn more about the concept of shocks to society, we suggest you look at the book *Future Shock* by Alvin Toffler. It came out in 1970 and defined a *future shock* as "a certain psychological state of individuals and entire societies. The shortest definition for the term in the book is a personal perception of 'too much change in too short a period of time.'" (Wikipedia)

So, what kind of shocks could be down the road? They could be economic downturns—like the stock market crash of 1929 that lasted until the manufacturing required for World War II pulled us out, or the banking crisis that caused the Great Recession of 2008. There could be future medical emergencies; the Centers for Disease Control tells us that there are viruses that exist that could lead to further pandemics very soon.

The Ability to Survive

Charles Darwin, 161 years ago, in his landmark 1859 book, *The Origin of Species*, showed that those species that *adapt* best to their changing environment have the best chance of surviving, while those who *do not adapt* do not generally make it. Darwin wrote, "It is not the strongest of the species that survives, nor the most intelligent that survives. It is the one that is the most adaptable to change."

We have adopted that concept and applied it to business when we advise company presidents on what they need to do next! Remember, since *Fortune* magazine came out with the Fortune 500 in 1955, they have had to replace 429 of the original 500 companies because even though they were large, they did not adapt to a continually changing economic landscape. The good news for smaller companies is that pivoting can be easier and quicker.

In 2020, as small business coaches, we were dealing with an unprecedented economic situation. For the first time since 2007 and 2008, the economy we were a part of was in an economic recession. Add to that, the downturn was immediate, caused by a worldwide pandemic. This downturn was not unforeseen. The normal economic cycle indicators saw it coming on the horizon. It's just that the horizon came months or years faster than expected. This left one needing the answer to a big question for any business: How are you going to pivot your marketing program to fit the current economy and the new paradigm which will follow?

In fact, how are you going to pivot your business during COVID-19 we asked? What could you do to ensure the survival of your business?

Lessons from COVID-19

As a small business owner, no matter how you defined your sales community, from local to global, there was a definite change in your community—a change in how your community related to itself and its members. There was a huge change in how your community saw your business.

The first thing that changed was buying habits. Normally we teach that there is a two-part question you must get a prospect to answer to make the sale. That question is "Why buy from me? and Why buy from me instead of my competitors?" The argument you must make is: "Here, let me tell you why." A third option, which has always existed, but under normal times did not often come into play, became more prevalent. That question was, "Should you buy at all?"

To successfully pivot a business during COVID-19 the business owner had to answer that question first to attract attention.

It began in the larger marketplaces. Automotive manufacturers Ford, Chrysler, and Toyota all say some version of, "If, during this time you need a vehicle . . ." instead of leading with the features and benefits of their model. They led with no payments for a certain amount of time. Why not take advantage of getting a deal on a car, now? This is right out of their "how to sell cars during a recession" playbook. Automotive vending machine company Carvana offered contactless delivery of your vehicle.

Pizza delivery chains like Dominos and Papa John's talked about how they would deliver your pizza without having ever touched it instead of talking about the value they brought? They answered that third question first. Both examples, automotive companies and pizza delivery companies, were relying on the fact that you, the consumer, would remember their years of previous feature/benefit advertising. One other affirmation of this strategy is that Pizza Hut, which did not offer delivery options, just had a quarter with sales down 11% and their largest franchisee partner declared bankruptcy.

How to Pivot

So, what did we recommend that our clients do to pivot a business during COVID-19? In short, get used to a few new rules. Here they were.

First, we told our clients to look at their customer base. Decide what the customer needed from them. And, just as important, how would they be able to deliver what the customer needed. Restaurants were the first to figure this out because they were not able to seat their clients in their establishments. Take Out banners appeared in front of a couple of dozen restaurants in our small town of Sedona. Our doctor's office began using Zoom for appointments.

At Yuloff Creative, we had to pivot all our events from in-person to virtual. In a short three-week arc in March, we went from our usual in-person three-day Small Business Breakthrough Bootcamp the first weekend, and pivoted the second weekend to an in-person, two-day bootcamp with follow-up calls to the attendees who had questions. For the event the last weekend, we pivoted again and did a two-day completely virtual bootcamp because by then, we could not see exposing our attendees to a possible virus. Each hotel we used saw an 80% drop in reservations in that twenty-one-day period.

A second pivot that we recommended was to embrace the era of personal distancing.

Perhaps obviously, personal distancing will continue to have some impact. Even as COVID-19 declines, it will take a long time for things to get back to normal. I remember that after the January 1994 Northridge Earthquake, we found that for months we did not travel to see clients in the north end of the San Fernando Valley. In the north was where most of the damage occurred. We were gun shy since our house was just two miles south of the epicenter. This time the entire world was the epicenter, and everyone was in the middle of it. When will we all, collectively, finally travel North? The answer is: when we pivot.

But your business had to make money, so needed to change the sales and marketing strategy that we were using just a short while before.

To pivot your business during COVID-19, you had to embrace your digital marketplace.

For some of you reading this there was a no-big-deal reaction, while others had an oh-no-that's-a-big-deal reaction. Each business owner had a different comfort level when it came to the digital marketplace. Here are five examples many used.

We know a business lawyer in Sherman Oaks, California who saw this as an opportunity. Keven Steinberg of Steinberg Law set up his practice as a boutique practice that could suddenly and easily compete with large law firms who have yet to figure out how to work remotely. Those firms are used to wooing a client with face-to-face meetings (and maybe paying for parking). Steinberg was able to work remotely with a high level of security for his clients.

The same goes for a business printer, Peacock Print Co. Mary Johnson had never relied on using a store front location. She was able to compete far more easily than her retail location land-locked competitors. By going digital, she was able to continue operating at a profit.

The same is true for a real estate client who could no longer hold open houses. He was one of the very first to use Facebook Lives and video virtual tours as his business pivot.

A financial planning firm, Freedman Crossett Financial Services in Cottonwood, Arizona found out quickly that her clients did not need to make the trip to see her in person or have her come to them. Cindy Crossett made it a point of being in phone contact with every customer. She used online video conferencing to meet with current and potential clients. She also provided virtual lunch-and-learns for people in her target markets.

That does not mean you can go full steam ahead without being very careful with your business pivots. Angie Lozano of Angie's House, a non-profit group of low-income homes, has found that she had to take extra steps before she could allow a new resident to move in. Luckily, she had worked for two years to prepare her business to be in a position to be more selective. The message is universal for many business owners; protect your business before moving forward.

One ubiquitous business pivot due to COVID-19 was the use of video conferencing.

With video conferencing software like FreeConferenceCalling, GoToMeeting, Zoom, Skype, and even FaceTime, a small business could still schedule and hold virtual meetings with staff, customers, prospects, and everyone else important to the business. It was very beneficial to build relationships. Even if we could not be belly-to-belly we could still be face-to-face.

While many of your customers were staying at home, they were spending hours online and looking at their devices. This was a great time to accelerate digital marketing strategies. This includes your blogs, your social media, email marketing, and even digital ads. And many people have been reluctant to leave the convenience of shopping that way.

The next pivot we recommended was to educate your prospects by offering virtual classes and education.

We know one business owner, who ran at least two virtual networking events a week. He gathered several business owners and they held a mastermind session to solve each of their challenges.

Throughout the world, every classroom, every industry conference and most certainly every convention was shut down or postponed. But your clients and prospects still wanted the opportunity to network with peers and learn about business. That's why we launched our own online series of webinars. You can do the same and show off your expertise in the industry.

This pivot helped to fill the knowledge gap with virtual classes or events, educational videos on YouTube, and each social media platform as well as blogging on websites. It continues to be a great return on investment. Now is still the time for you to bump up the amount of time you invest to get published in various media outlets. Every time you are published, you enjoy an opportunity to build your reputation of expertise in your industry.

It is the rare company who did not have their sales process changed in some way. Even online retailers had to work with their shipping companies to be extra certain their shipments would safely arrive on time. If you relied on being in-person to make sales, you had to drastically change your process.

As a result, many companies, ours included, began using more printed sales tools. We highlighted our ability to give free consultations. When we made phone calls, we added an important twist; at the beginning of those calls, we took a few minutes to connect on a human level. That is still a practice that has value. Direct mail and phone calls can play a large part of what you should do to attract your ideal and most profitable clients.

And as we take the best lessons from a very challenging time, and as we continue to pivot as our business needs require it, you will find that your sales funnel will continue to fill and eventually, we will all head North again.

Your Action Item ❏

Look back at your business and what you did during the Covid-19 pandemic. Make a list of what worked and what did not.

Were there things you did *before* the pandemic that you have stopped doing? Would it make sense to bring those back?

This is a time to do a bit of thinking and plan what to do in case and when something happens next.

* * *

When we coach small business owners, we constantly discuss the changes they can make in their marketing path. Some are large, most are small. If you want to discuss your list, reach out to us at www.HowToGetThereFaster.com.

Epilogue

Final Thought to (Over)Think About

Napoleon Hill said, "The person who does more than what they are paid for will soon be paid for more than what they do."

We often wonder how many people later regret telling us, "that's too expensive, I'll figure it out for myself." We will quite often keep them on our mailing list for our monthly positive-message greeting card that we send out to our list. *

Most often when we go to look them up, sadly, they never did. We see websites that have the same mistakes and incomplete pages or broken links. We see social media pages that have not been posted to in weeks. We see blogs with dates, no videos or testimonials, and dozens of easy fixes, for us, that were never figured out.

We often wonder how much time and money they spent over that period instead of hiring us to work for them, think for them, create for them, educate, and advise them, figure it all out and hand it to them.

This came up recently when we heard from a woman who was looking for a new job. We had talked with her boss a few months previously and laid out some steps that he could take right away to finally make his employment agency successful after two years of effort. He gave the usual excuses for why he wasn't ready to get started.

At that meeting, I glanced at Sharyn. We knew. We recognized the tone, the facial response. He wasn't ready. There would be too much change for him. It wasn't the investment amount—it rarely is. We price our coaching for this very type of client; we make it affordable but always remind them that they have skin in the game and together we have work to do.

It was sad to hear from her that her employer had never done any of the things we told him we would hold his hand through to save his company. As

119

I have heard Sharyn ask people all the time: "How badly do you want it?"

There is a video we play all the time that features Eric Thomas—an incredible motivational speaker. It's called, "When You Want It As Bad As You Want to Breathe."

We recommend you watch it. Ask yourself these questions:
1. When it comes to sales, how badly do I want it?
2. What am I selling?
3. Is my list big enough? It needs to be so large that when someone says *no* to you, it does not devastate you or slow you down.
4. Am I getting into sales opportunities every day?
5. Do I want it more than I want to breathe (figuratively, of course)?

So why *do* people buy from you? We ask that a lot on our free get-your-business-focused calls. And most small business owners are confused in their answers. They don't really know. If you don't know, here is a little coaching tip: Ask them. It's a very scary question, yes, but you will be very glad you did.

Here are some ways we recommend that you use in your sales process to encourage your prospects to buy from you:
1. You can offer lots of social proof—telling stories of results, testimonials and awards is a great way to do this. One of *our* favorite stories has to do with a nonprofit in Cottonwood, AZ that was a coaching client for three years. For about a year, we suggested that she make one little change in her process, but it would take a leap of faith. The owner took the suggestion and added $40,000 profit to her bottom line the next year.

2. Free knowledge. We are asked all the time: "Sharyn and Hank, why do you give away so much knowledge for free?" We feel that the more people benefit from what we offer for free, the more they will say to themselves, "Wow, if they're this good for free, they must be incredible when I invest in their coaching." This is another leap of faith but try it and report back to us.

3. Stop selling—well, stop being salesy. Showing you care, asking the right questions and sharing the transformation that will come in their business and life have got to be added to your repertoire, or sales process, to stand out in the marketplace. Fill your sales funnel full by caring.

4. *Keep* selling—the sale is not done when the prospect says yes. We were on a scheduled thirty-minute coaching call with a client who

is a coach. At the bottom of the hour, as we were digging deep into something that was really challenging her, she said "I realize we are getting to the end of our call, can you give me some things to do to fix this?" Both Sharyn and I responded at the same time "Don't worry about it, let's keep working." In another fifteen minutes we had solved the challenge and she had direction. This happens all the time. Our goal is to give our clients so much value that when it comes time to renew their program, it's an easy *yes*.

5. In one of our other books, *The Marketing Checklist for Sales*, we discussed the Cajun concept of a lagniappe (LAN' yop). It means something given as a bonus or extra gift. That concept guides our coaching.

6. We use this concept of lagniappe with prospects, too. Quite often, when we tell a prospect we will send them a particular special report or link to a video on a topic they need, we will add one of our books to the email, or something else we think they would find useful.

7. Tell stories. Share your struggle. Talk about your journey. When you can do this without being too salesy, this will build trust and show you to be a credible source of knowledge. Here's your coaching tip: Look at your "About" page on your website. Is it . . . corporate? Written in third person? Or is it in first person, telling your story with your photo and a welcome video? Let people get to know you. We had one coach that we worked with for a while and, though we loved the information we received, a true value, one reason we did not renew was that we never felt we knew the real person. There was always a mask that kept clients at arm's length. It's our opinion that wearing your heart on your sleeve is an overall positive benefit for you and your clients.

This brings us to the end of book number eight. We very much appreciate your investing your valuable time to learn from us. Now is the time to go through your answers to the action items throughout the book and make your plan. If you have not done that yet, begin now with the items below.

Be well! And remember our slogan: If everything happens for a reason, be the reason things happen.

Your Action Item ❏
What ways will you use to acquire and keep clients? What lagniappe can you offer from your business?

Your Action Item ❑

Create a list of marketing tactics you want to implement. We suggest a list of twelve. Of those twelve, what are the three most important? Put them on the top. Of those three, what is the *I-must-do-this-now item*? That is the one to do first. Then move on to the next two (of the top three). The idea is to add one of these to your marketing program each month for a year. Don't add them all at once or you will become *overwhelmed* by *overthinking* and as the title of this book says, we want you to avoid that.

Play the long game. It's why our coaching programs are a year at a time because it takes time to get your marketing on the right track.

You can do it!

* * *

* If you would like to see how this system works email us your *mailing address* and we will send you a couple. Email to Info@YuloffCreative.com and put *"add me to the card list"* in the subject line. Remember, it's a *mail* address, *not* an email address. These are real greeting cards.

Our Story—Our Mission
Our Vision—Our Whys

Sharyn's Origin Story

Although I was born in Los Angeles, my parents divorced when I was three-years-old and my mom and I moved to Israel to build a life and family with my stepdad.

The summer I was seven, we visited Los Angeles and I re-met my dad. I returned to LA the following summer to visit with my dad and his new wife.

The Yom Kippur War broke out when I was nine-years-old which freaked me out. I begged my mom to allow me to move back to live with my dad, in LA, where there weren't bombs going off in our back yard and over the radio.

Although I was told my dad wouldn't treat me as nicely when I was there full time, it seemed worth the risk to not be worried about bombs.

Unfortunately, my mom and her friends were more correct than they had anticipated. The first ten months of life with dad were typical. Although not every day was rainbows and unicorns, it was a good and safe life.

However, once my younger brother was born, my dad's coping skills were over-tasked. The least frustration sent him into a rage, and he sent my head crashing into our apartment wall. As if that wasn't enough punishment, I then had to clean the blood off the wall.

Although I searched for a more suitable father figure, all I found were sexual predators. My dad's friends, a teacher, and my best friend's stepdad.

I was molested by nine father figures from the time I was ten until I was sixteen) I know that statistically you may also be an abuse survivor or know someone who is.

Even with that traumatic childhood history, we've been married for almost thirty years and have been business coaches together for over ten.

My journey to business coach: If you know Hank's story, then you know that he started this company on his own, thanks to his mom's prompting.

Meanwhile, I was working at the time as office and HR (human resources) manager in entertainment and financial services for small-business organizations. My last role was as HR director for a large (300 employees), multi-national, 2D to 3D film conversion house. During my tenure, I suffered a work-related injury and was on disability for a year.

During that year, I was home (in between physical therapy appointments) and got to eavesdrop on Hank's conversations with his clients.

Until that year, I thought he was The Marketing Guy and believed that I didn't know much about marketing. However, by listening in on his conversations, I came to realize that his conversations were very similar to the ones I had been having in my HR office. This realization led me to the revelation that HR is really internal marketing (unless placing a job posting). For more on this, I invite you to read our book entitled *Small Business Human Resources Secrets*.

At the end of the year of disability, one of Hank's clients hired us to help grow her small business using Hank's knowledge of marketing and sales, and my background in human resources and back-office systems.

At the end of the contract, we decided to continue to combine forces for the benefit of our small business clients.

It's been a great ride and we are so grateful we took the leap of faith together!

Hank's Origin Story

Let me tell you a quick story about my very first experience with how small business owners were often taught how to do what they do but not how to market what they do.

I had just begun working for my college newspaper, *The Daily Aztec* at San Diego State, selling advertising space. On a cold call I went into the very first Subway sandwich shop in California, not knowing it was a franchise. After the owner explained that there would soon be a bunch of these shops in our town, he said that other than some possible ads, the company was leaving his advertising programs entirely up to him, and he was confused by it. He was, he said, a sandwich guy not a marketing guy.

I struggled with the idea that these *adults* (I was barely twenty-years-old) had no real concept about marketing and were looking to *ME*, an advertising *student* to guide their company that they had invested their life savings to open. How was that possible? And he was not an outlier. I had a few dozen accounts that were completely looking to me to save their livelihoods. And I could not let them down.

It was during the two years of being the top salesperson, and then becoming the advertising manager, that I realized I had focused my dream of using my public relations, advertising and economics degrees to help small business owners. I had a talent for it and following that dream would help thousands of families have a better life.

Our Company's Origin

Our company began inauspiciously. When going around the Thanksgiving table, sharing what we were thankful for, my Mom noticed that I was not very happy being one of the sales managers for a national company.

I told her I was not. That there were several things which made the job a *job* instead of a career. I told her that there was less and less client contact, and that was what I was best at— helping businesses get more business. She looked at me with a look I was very familiar with—the let's-fix-this-now look. And she asked a very specific question: "What would it take for you to open your own business?"

I took a moment and replied that "the only thing I would really need is a fax machine, Mom, since the one I have belongs to the company and I would have to return it. I have everything else but a name."

Mom turned to my Dad and said, "Write him a check." And looked at me and said, "Come up with a name." It is those specific moments which we think back on that change the direction of our lives which are so special.

That was over twenty-seven years ago. In that time, Promotionally Minded, the name chosen from a long list, has grown in its marketing offerings from promotional products to small marketing projects, to advice on public relations, to complete marketing plans where often we are the ad-hoc marketing department for small companies under our own TheCompanyMarketing-Plan.com product name.

It has not been without growing pains—a couple of recessions and a "learning moment" or three has cost us dearly, but those setbacks and delays have also made us smarter and a better advisor to our clients. In fact, each time we have gone from business cruise control to business expansion, we have had the feeling that all entrepreneurs have: Time to just jump out of the nest and fly.

Quite often, we get put into a box of what people think *marketing people* do. The challenge is, so many salespeople, printers and graphic artists, or website developers say they are marketing people. Most of them focus on one part of a business, like making their website or shooting their videos. In other words, they all do some marketing, but a very small part of the overall—a marketing department—that most small business owners need but cannot afford to have on staff.

We fill that role.

Holistically, we begin at the beginning with the small business owner. We look at where they have been, where they want to be and most important for you, what you want your life to look like as your business moves forward.

Then, we figure out who their best target clients are to meet their goals, what are the messages they need to reach those clients and what tactics we will need to use to get there. *Most* people who say they are in marketing incorrectly start with that last step.

The bonus you get when you work with us is that we are a team. Our business backgrounds are very different but cover the four areas most business owners would like expert help with: sales, human resources, public speaking (in other words, how to convey your message) and marketing.

We're your marketing department that is virtually down the hall at an investment that is a tiny fraction of what you would need to invest if you had all those people full-time on staff. What makes us different is that if you had those people on staff, most of them are worried about keeping their jobs, first, and your business succeeding second. Our only job is to make you successful.

The latest jump, and the biggest one by far, was the creation of the Small Business Breakthrough Bootcamps. We have always told our clients that being in a *category of one* was the way to move yourself up the success pyramid, and for us, this is a definite trailblazing experience. The excitement of taking all that we have learned, and keep learning in an ever-changing technological setting, and sharing it all in small groups of entrepreneurs is exhilarating. The business owners who find us are true experts in their fields, and it is our job to help them deftly overcome competitors who either have had a marketing head start or, in some cases, are just flat outspending them. One client said that we approach our objectives like "marketing tornados with a David vs. Goliath chip on our shoulders."

Pre-COVID pandemic, when we did them in person, we would put your marketing plan together for you in two and a half days. Post pandemic, we changed them into a one-day event. We offer the program to create comprehensive marketing plans for our attendees. If you're reading this, we invite you (your free ticket is at PlanYourMarketing.com) to experience the kind of marketing intensive bootcamp which will not only reenergize you, but it will reenergize your *sales*, will make your head spin with incredible marketing ideas, and send you out as a new Goliath in your marketplace.

Our Mission Statement

For our clients, we are the masters of their marketing message. We deliver their message directly to the eyes of their customer. Through superior coaching, our clients stay out of the habit of being in the habit.

We believe that when your business exists to serve your life, when marketing your business, you will always be reminded to begin with the end in mind.

We are enemies of average.

Our Vision Statement

Small business owners that are good at what they do deserve a marketing plan that will increase their relevancy and raise their profits. We will create programs that make a positive difference to each client. We are the coaching team small business owners can turn to when they need their marketing questions answered honestly and accurately. We will continuously offer a much better than expected value for a fair investment.

Our Core Values

1. Empowering small business owners to make their business serve the life they want to lead.
2. Employing persistence to reach goals and gain wisdom.
3. To be faithful, reliable, and loyal to friends, family, and community.

Hank's why is taken from my religion. There is a saying "Tikun Olam" which when roughly translated means to heal the world. To me it is to build community without taking credit. The concept was familiar to me through the news for years. The concept of delivering the envelope was solidified for me when I heard Kody Bateman tell the story of how his brother had tragically died in a work accident and his neighbors all gathered to complete the landscaping around the new home that he had just moved his family in to. My why is to be a deliverer of the sometimes metaphorical and sometimes the actual envelope that carries inside the answer to a challenge that vexes a person, a family, a community. Sometimes it is cash. One time it was a banner that was ripped down from a church. Our lives gain more and more meaning, the more we give back.

The Answers to Questions
We Hear All the Time

What do you do?
When answering the question "what do you do" Hank references his raccoon power to say that we are problem solvers for our small business owning clients. That is because the racoon is the problem solver. People with the raccoon as their totem are problem solvers who leave no stone unturned in their quest for truth and solutions. When it comes to sales, marketing, and running their business, we work for them, think for them, create for them, and figure it all out.

What can you do for me (the person asking)?
That is a very common question. And no matter who asks it, my answer begins with "it depends." Each of our clients are different and every day, we solve a variety of problems for each of them. We have made so many course corrections for them, some small, some large, that our menu of services has reached over a dozen pages. What part of your business is troubling you?

What makes you come alive?
It happens when we look at what a client is doing to market themselves, the methods and effort, and to offer an answer. And they get it. And we immediately get to work together to fix it.

In the greater world, we want to share our good fortune with those who are in need. Some tithe to a church, we tithe to humanity.

What are your innate strengths?
Telling truth to power.
Making other's ideas better. Improvement through augmentation.
Creating content from scratch and editing existing copy.

Planning, seeing the big picture for and organizing an event.

An affiliative leadership style where everyone is connected and works well together.

Where do you add the greatest value?

In a consultative situation seeing the weak spots in a situation.

Short-term, one-shot injections of change.

Long term, series of corrections successfully achieving long term goals.

How will you measure your life?

Knowing that we made a difference in our communities. That we left them in a better place than they would have been if we did not act.

Other Books By Sharyn And Hank Yuloff
Naked Book Publishing

49 Stupid Things People Do with Business Cards . . .
And How to Fix Them

The Marketing Checklist
80 Simple Ways to Master Your Marketing

The Marketing Checklist 2
49 More Simple Ways to Master Your Marketing

The Marketing Checklist 3
The Hows and Whys of Social Media

The Marketing Checklist for Human Resources
*The Right Way to Hire, Cultivate, and Terminate Employees,
All While Improving Your Marketing*

The Marketing Checklist for Sales
49 Easy Ways to Improve Your Sales for Professionals

Partners in Everything
*Your Couples' Guide to Running a Successful
Business Without Ruining Your Life*

And more in the pipeline as well!

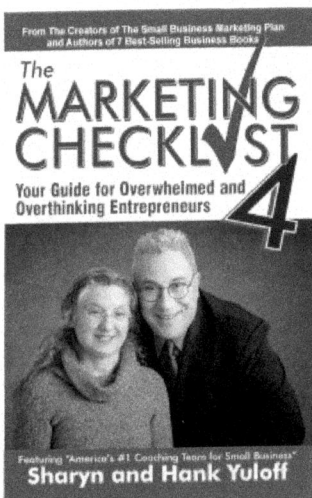

www.ingramcontent.com/pod-product-compliance
Lightning Source LLC
Chambersburg PA
CBHW050509210326
41521CB00011B/2382